AF553459

Published by:
Tilak Wasan
DISCOVERY PUBLISHING HOUSE PVT. LTD.
4383/4B, Ansari Road, Darya Ganj
New Delhi-110 002 (India)
Phone : +91-11-23279245, 43596064-65
Fax : +91-11-23253475
E-mail : discoverypublishinghouse@gmail.com
sales@discoverypublishinggroup.com
parul.wasan@gmail.com
web : www.discoverypublishinggroup.com

First Edition: **2013**

ISBN: 978-93-5056-303-8

Service Marketing in Cellular Phone

Printed at:
Aditi Fine Art Press
Delhi

Preface

Today we live in a service economy. The perception of service marketing focuses on selling the services in the best interest of users/ customers. Telecommunication services play an incremental role in the multi-dimensional development activities. A well functioning telecommunications network is an essential component of economic infrastructure. The application of marketing principles in the telecommunication service sector is the main thing in the service marketing. The modern innovative marketing principles would help the organization in improving the quality of their services.

India as Asia's third largest economy is adding at least one million new mobile phone users every month. The perception income of the people and urbanization in India is growing at a faster rate. The income level in the rural area is rising due to robust agricultural output.

Cell Phone being viewed as a common man's phone now, there will be better scope for telecom and related services in India. The important service providers in GSM market are Bharati Camp, BSNL, Hutchinson camp (Vodaphone), Idea Group, BPL Group, Spice group, Escotel group, Reliance Group, MTNL and others. The number of subscribers is increasing from 12,688 million in 2003 to 37,402 millions in 2005 and even far more now. There is a cut throat competition in GSM market. Each service provider has become more quality conscious and also customers centric. The success of the corporates in GSM market depends upon their ability to satisfy their customers. Hence, the present study focuses on analysing the service quality of service providers, service quality gap, customer satisfaction, customer loyalty and customers switching behaviour in the GSM market.

The present study on cellular phone service markets is presented in seven Chapters.

Chapter I includes the Introduction, Need for the Study, Statement of the Problem, Review of Previous Studies, Proposed Research Model, Objectives of the Study, Methodology of the Study, Limitations and Scheme of the Report.

Chapter II deals with the conceptual framework of the Study.

Chapter III includes the theoretical frame work of the Study. It highlights the cellular phone service market in India, customer base, market share of various service providers and their marketing strategies.

Chapter IV examines the various Profiles of the Customers, Source of Information about the service provider, Factors leading to choose the service provider, Association between Profile of Customer and their perception on factors and discriminant factors among the young and elder customers.

Chapter V covers the various service quality factors (SQFs) Level of expectation and perception on SQFs, Service quality gaps, Customer satisfaction on their service providers, Discriminant SQFs among the satisfiers and dissatisfiers; Young and elder customers; and Impact of SQFs on the customers' satisfaction.

Chapter VI includes the Switching Behaviours, Factors leading to Switching, Impact of switching factors on switching intentions, Customer loyalty, Impact of switching factors on customer loyalty, Linkage between SQFs, overall attitude and customers' Loyalty.

Chapter VII summarises the Findings, Conclusions, Policy implications and directions for future research.

A descriptive research design was followed to fulfill the objectives of the research. The study was conducted by the researcher with the help of pre tested and structured interview schedule. The study was viewed on two dimensional analysis namely service providers and customers segment. The collected primary data was processed with the help of appropriate statistical tools to fulfill the objectives of the study. This is the first book which describes all quality aspects of cellular phone service marketing and it will be very much helpful to the research scholars for carrying out research work in various aspects of telecommunication services. In fact this book will be an ideal guide to the researchers.

We are grateful to express our deep sense of thanks to:

Dr. M. Jezer Jebanesan, Principal of Scott Christian College (Autonomous), Nagercoil for making available the needed facilities to complete the research work.

We place our sincere gratitude to the Head of the Department of Commerce ***Dr. M. Wilson*** and all the staff members for their encouragement and help.

We would like to express our deep sense of thanks to ***Dr. X. Antony Thanaraj,*** Associate Professor, Department of Commerce, Scott Christian College (Autonomous), Nagercoil for his valuable guidance and suggestions.

We sincerely thank ***Mr. P. Jegan***, Lecturer in the Department of Commerce, Scott Christian College (Autonomous), Nagercoil for his valuable support in all possible ways.

We express our sincere thanks to Manonmaniam Sundaranar University Library, Tirunelveli, Madurai Kamaraj University Library, Madurai, Centre for Development Studies Library, Trivandrum, Commerce Department Library and main library of Scott Christian College (Autonomous), Nagercoil.

We express our deep sense of gratitude to Lord, the Almighty for His Mercy and Grace, which we have received bountifully and in abundance, throughout this course of study.

We are also thankful to Discovery Publishing House Private Ltd., New Delhi for publishing this book.

Dr. M. Edwin Gnanadhas
M. Rasheed

Contents

Introduction and Design of the Study

Introduction

The Telecom Sector is one of the fastest growing Sectors. It offers three categories of services, namely, fixed line, wireless and cellular service. The cellular service is called as mobile service because of its nature of usage. There are two types of mobile service networks (a) Global System for Mobile (GSM) and (b) Code Division Multiple Access (CDMA). The band width of GSM varies from CDMA. The study revolves around the operators of GSM service. The service industry supports the natural economy with more than 55 per cent growth rate. Its contribution to the Gross Domestic Product (GDP) is less than 20 per cent. To hasten the growth and strengthen the Indian Economy, it is essential to study the nature of service offered. The study is enlightened to the service quality of GSM networks.

After the liberalization of the Indian Telecom Sector, 1994, the Indian cellular market witnessed a higher growth in cellular services. By 2005, there were a total of 12 players in the market with the five major players being Bharati Televentures Limited (Bharati). Bharat Sanchar Nigam Limited (BSNL), Hutchinson-Eassar Limited (Hutch), Idea Cellular Limited (Idea) and Reliance Indian Mobile (RIM). All the players except RIM offered services based on the Global system for mobile (GSM) technology. RIM provided services based on Code Division Multiple Access (CDMA) technology as well as GSM. As competition in the telecom area intensified, service providers took new initiatives to customers. Prominent among these were celebrity, endorsements, loyalty rewards, discount coupons, business solutions and talk time services. The most important consumer segments in the Cellular industry were the youth segment and the business class segment. The youth segment was the largest and fastest growing segment and was therefore targeted by cellular service providers. Hence all the service providers concentrate on more service quality to attract new customers in GSM market.

Need for the Study

As market growth slows on as market becomes more competitive, service providers are more likely to attempt to maintain their market share by focussing on retaining existing customers. Customer retention has been advocated as an easier and more reliable source of superior performance (Reichheld and Sasser, 1990)[1]. To improve customer retention, service providers initiate variety of services, including programs on customer satisfaction (Jones and Sasser, 1995)[2], complaint management. (Fornell and Wernerfelt, 1987)[3] and loyalty (Dowling and Uncles, 1997)[4]. In understanding customer satisfaction, researchers paid attention to the management of service quality (Rust and Zahorit, 1993)[5]; developing strategies to meet current expectations, and explaining the impact of service quality on customer satisfaction (Zeithaml *et al.*, 1996)[6]. In explaining, the link between service quality, customer satisfaction and customer loyalty, only a few studies have examined the factors leading to customer satisfaction and switching. The increasing competition in Indian spectrum of mobile industry is reducing the price of service and customers are bombarded with various services and changing tariff plans. Brand Loyalty function, like insulator for brands, which prevent competitor to grab their customers. Customer satisfaction is a decisive component for creating loyal customer base. Hence the present study has made an attempt to study the linkage between service quality, customer satisfaction and customer loyalty in mobile phone service industry in India.

Statement of the Problem

Cellular mobile phone communication is a tool for the beneficial use of individual including professional and businessman. Though the cellular operators have been rendering services to its customers throughout India, it has become a target of controversy due to many reasons, such as, excess billing, disconnection while talking, cross talk while talking, high cost handset and high operating cost. Recently, the cellular operators are subject to comments and criticism for various reasons. Their services are not only commendable, but also satisfying to the consumers to some extent. The important threats of cellular mobile service market in India are high costs of service provision, low-income among the people cannot be offered to replicate expensive telecom infrastructure, political instability, Chinas early liberalization, threats from WLL service providers and also from satellite phones. The customer's expectations and knowledge of the mobile phone service are also increasing at the other hand. Hence the service providers are facing challenges, not only from the competitors, but also from their customers. The consistent updation of the service quality is the only measure to regain the existing customers and attract the new customers in order to increase their subscriber base.

Review of Previous Studies

The review of previous studies are summarized below:

Cellular market in India

Srikant (2006)[7] revealed that the strength of the Cellular mobile industry in India has a huge wireless subscriber potential, and is the fastest growing mobile market in the world. Consumers are ready to pay for cutting edge services, cheap labour to attract foreign investments, telecom professionals, telecom infrastructure, relaxation of government rules and regulations for foreign participants and lowest tariffs in the world.

Srivastava *et al.*, (2006)[8] pointed out that the price plays an significant role in growing or emerging market like that in the telecom sector. For telecom companies to do service and be competitive or even glow, they continuously need to provide customers extra value added features, high quality services at competitive price, so that customers do not switch to other operators. Although the companies are in the growth phase, they cannot afford to be complacent and need to continuously innovative through aggressive pricing, attractive schemes and superior service to retain and expand customer strength.

Revathi and Padmavathi (2005)[9] identified that majority of the subscribers are following the post-paid system. Their switching tendency to other cellular service is more. Shashi Kumar and Chauley (2007)[10] felt that the consumer satisfaction on mobile service depends on the demographic characteristics of the respondents. The deep positive impact of the mobile services on social changes has been identified. The future of mobile services is very bright. It is also concluded that the mobile service providers should exercise due care before introducing new services.

Banumathy and Kalaivani (2006)[11]revealed that majority of respondents form the services provided by the mobile services. The important reasons for choosing cell phone are facility to identify the missed calls, more convenience and low cost. The level of satisfaction among the consumers is found to be as higher in the case of Aircel and BSNL, whereas, it is lesser in the case of Reliance and Airtel.

Alok and Sirohi (2006)[12] found that the cellular service providers provide quality of services to their customers. It will also help the new entrants to formulate the strategies by following the results of existing companies. The study can also help the cellular companies in determining their service level by comparing it with the expected service level of the customers. Switching from one service to another because of service and cost of the existing services.

The price offered by the service providers plays an important role in switching from one operator to another. Hence, they concluded that the service providers can not only command market leadership based on quality product, but also has to be matched with attractive pricing.

Francis and Lydia (2005)[13] mentioned that the factors influencing the migration to post paid from prepaid among the cell phone users are economic, attractive schemes, reference group influence, limited usage and advertisement.

Consumer's perception on Cellular Services

Consumer behavior refers to the act of consuming goods or services. The review of consumer behaviour in the cellular industry is summarized below:

Selvaraj and Ganesan (2005)[14] found that majority of the cell phone users are satisfied with the mobile services but they opined that the billing pattern is not at the satisfactory level. They perceived mobile services as a cheaper mode of communication. They are satisfied with the advertisement given by mobile services.

Daxa (2005)[15] revealed that the important requirements for telephone among the customers are common communication and business requirements. Majority of the customers perceived that the services are excellent. The important reasons for dropping the services are high rate, lack of network and lack of coverage in rural area. The level of education, age and income are not significantly associated with the perception on the service provided by the Telecom Companies.

Vijay Kumar and Priya (2006)[16] found that the important factors influencing the satisfaction derived by the subscribers of Airtel network are the clarity of signals, availability of plan options, call charges and the activation formalities. Majority of the respondents opined that Airtel offers plenty of value added services, convenient plan options, activation formalities and moderate call charges. There is a significant association between the profile of respondents and their attitude towards the services offered by Airtel.

Chao and Gupta (1995)[17] revealed that a higher level of education can be expected to increase the degree of consumers' involvement when buying a sophisticated product like a mobile handset. Educated people are more likely to engage in more meaningful search for information and production evaluation, thus, rating some factors like country of origin as important in order to make rational buying decisions.

Hui and Zhou, (2002)[18] reported that country of origin may affect consumers in various ways such as their perception of product quality, their perception of foreign goods and products, purchase intention and purchase value.

Ahmed *et al.,* (2002)[19] claimed that extrinsic cues play an significant role in reducing perceived risk, which is intensely related to purchase intention and product evaluation. The role of country of origin as an external factor that influences consumer behaviour has been appreciated in most consumer behaviour models.

Ibrahim and Pajaree (2006)[20] revealed that country of origin effects are an insubstantial factor in consumer evaluation of mobile handsets. Other product factors, such as, disability, design, features, brand and price were perceived by consumers in both countries as more important, than country of origin. The respondents were also found to be more interested in the made in label and have a strong preference towards products manufactured in particular countries.

Customers Attitude towards Mobile Telecommunication Services

The customer satisfaction is defined as the perceived values among users of mobile phone services. The reviews related to the customers attitude are illustrated below.

Balasubramanian *et al.,* (2002)[21] identified that the unique intrinsic attributes mentioned by the end users are unhindered time and space attributes of the mobile phone. The extrinsic attributes are divided as direct and indirect network. Direct network is the effect of the size, speed and capacity of the network, whereas, indirect network is the effect originating from the information, transaction, or machine interactive services.

Raja *et al.,* (2006)[22] stated the product quality, product distribution, service supports, service personnel, information services and corporate brand equity are the integral factors influencing customer satisfaction of mobile handset end users. The successful adoption of the mobile handsets among the users can be attributed to unique features provided through product distribution and brand equity, and distinct features like, innovativeness, reachability and convenience. The highly satisfied cluster group predominantly consisted of Nokia and Sony Erickson handset users. Dissatisfaction was noticed among the cluster which consisted of Motorola and Samsung handset users.

Sashikala (2006)[23] examined the relationships between service quality and its related variables and also the desired qualities improve customer retention among the mobile service providers. The result implicates that customers set Reliability among the components of service quality as the important criterion to determine behavioural intention. Service quality includes elements, like coverage, connectivity and voice clarity which are strongly correlated with the technical limitation of the mobile subscriber network as well as service providers own infrastructure. The identified important discriminant service quality factors among the satisfied and the dissatisfied in the mobile phone services are reliability and responsiveness.

Chinnadurai and Kalpana (2006)[24] compared the different cellular services. The Aircel users considered that the sales promotion of the company is the important promotional strategy, whereas, among the Airtel and BPL users, these are advertisement and sales promotion. Among the BSNL and Reliance users, these factors are advertisement. The study also reveals that the Aircel and BPL are ranked first in the matter of cost and coverage, whereas, the Aircel and BSNL rated first and second the cost and facilities. The Reliance concentrates on the cost aspect and next the service aspect.

Service quality in Cellular Market

Wand and Lo (2002)[25] identified the relationship between the service quality factors, overall service quality, customer value, customer satisfaction and behavior intentions. The significant impact is identified between the tangibles, reliability on overall service quality; assurance and empathy on overall service quality, tangibles, empathy, network quality and customer sacrifice on customer value: reliability, assurance and net work quality on customer satisfaction and customer value and satisfaction on behaviour intentions.

Bloemer *et al.,* (1998) identified the base services in GSM sector are coverage of calling area, value-added services, customer support services, the supplier's services of the operator and services in campaigns. The study also identified the significant impact of perceived service quality in GSM sector on consumer loyalty.

Martin and Ibrahim (2006)[26] mentioned that the service quality of the electronic services is narrated by the confirmatory factor analysis into graphic quality, clarity, of layout, attractiveness of selection, information quality, base of use, technical quality, reliability, functional benefit and emotional benefit.

Service quality Gap Analysis

Clement (2005)[27] analysed the service quality gap in sixteen dimensions, namely, management perceptions, service quality strategy, service design, service gaps, quality supportive financial function, internal communication, integration, co-ordination, selection and training, service delivery, external communications, personnel's perceptions of customers' expectations, contact personnels perceptions of customers experiences, human element, consumer perceptions and service quality evaluation.

Zillur Rahman (2005)[28] identified the higher service quality gap in commercial banks as 'reliability' dimensions. The consumers' perception of service quality did not meet with their expectations. The higher service quality gap is identified in a few aspects of service quality, namely, customers feeling while interacting with the bank staff, pruning service at the promised time and employees instil confidence in customers.

Gani and Bhat (2003)[29] revealed that the service quality gap is lesser in foreign banks compared to that of Indian Banks. Our Banks are lagging behind in the matter of physical facilities, up-to-date equipment, communication, material, neatness of employees, prompt service, willingness of employees to help customers, convenient operating hours, customers' interest at the heart of employees and personal attention.

Customer Switching

Roos (2004)[30] identified the switching options are comparatively new to Telecommunication customers in the Nordic countries. This affects switching behaviour. The market has been turbulent for the same reasons, which in turn encourages low offers from new competitors. From the traditional Government owned telecommunications company's point of view, customers can only partly switch and therefore perceive the network to constitute switching barriers.

Wong and Hing (2002)[31] revealed that although there are two players in China's mobile phone market, the competition between them is more intense than ever. They compete not only in network quality by a large investment in network extension and upgrading, but also in customers retention and acquisition by direct and indirect price reduction. The service quality and customer satisfaction has significantly positive behaviour in direct price reduction. The service quality and customer satisfaction has significantly positive behaviour intention on customers and negative intention on their switching behaviour.

Anita *et al.*, (2005)[32] mentioned that the important reasons for non-switching from one service provider to another are the cost and energy involved in informing so many people about change in their number, confusion regarding the service offerings and complex tariff plans provided by other competitors, whereas, the reason for switching is dissatisfaction with their current service providers owing to the hidden costs and other factors.

Eventhough, there are so many previous studies related to consumers, preference of service provider, service quality in mobile phone service market, customer intention and switching behaviour in the market, there are only a few studies related to the marketing strategies in GSM and CDMA market on a comparative basis. Hence, the present study focuses on the market strategies of various service providers in GSM and CDMA market.

Customer loyalty in Cellular Phone Service Market

Bloomer et al., (1998)[33] identified that the switching cost as a crucial factor for customer loyalty in the market. Differentiation of the service will increase perceived switching cost. The change shifts competition in GSM sector from price and core services to value added services is used as a weapon to generate the customer loyalty.

Chada and Kapoor (2009)[34] found that there is positive association between the switching cost, service quality, customer satisfaction and customer loyalty. The customer satisfaction was found to be the test predictor of customer loyalty. The improvement in network quality, pricing value added services and switching costs contribute to increased loyalty and customer retention.

Geropott *et al.*, (2001)[35] analysed the relationship between customer satisfaction and loyalty in cellular mobile service market in Germany. They found that the three constructs, namely, customer satisfaction, customer loyalty and customer retention are different. Customer satisfaction derives customer loyalty, which in turn has an impact on customer retention.

Lee *et al.*, (2001)[36] examined the customer loyalty among the various customers segments in cellular mobile phone service market. They segmented the customer into economy, standard and mobile lovers on the basis of calling time. They found that the switching cost played a significant moderating role in the satisfaction-loyalty link for economy and standard groups.

Wang and Lo (2002)[37] pointed out that the network quality is one of the most important drivers of overall service quality and customer satisfaction. Customer perceived quality has a significantly positive impact on customers satisfaction and then their behaviour intentions.

Rana weera and Neely (2003)[38] developed a holistic model by incorporating constructs, such as, customer indifference and inertia into the retention model. Study showed price perception and indifference moderated the relationship between service perceptions and customer retention.

Kim *et al.*, (2004)[39] mentioned that the service quality positively affected customer satisfaction. Call quality is the most important issue that impacts customer satisfaction for mobile services. Customer satisfaction and switching barriers has positive impact on customer loyalty.

Palkar (2004)[40] analysed the determinants of customers' satisfaction and loyalty in mobile service market. The important determinants of these two are quality of service, price structure and value added services offered by the providers.

Ray and Sarkar (2006)[41] examined the influence of the brand name in customer loyalty. They identified that there is a significant positive impact of brand name of the service provider on the customer loyalty.

Selvarasu *et al.*, (2006)[42] identified that the important factors in influencing the customer satisfaction in GSM mobile service market are basic services, net work performance, value added services, recharging comfortability, customer care support and internet support.

Eventhough, there are so many studies related to the service quality of service providers in GSM market, customer satisfaction and customer loyalty in the GSM market, but only few studies are related with the linkage between the above said three concepts. But all these studies are related with the foreign countries. There is no exclusive study on the linkage between the service quality, customer satisfaction and customer loyalty in Indian context. Hence, the present study has made an attempt to fill up the research gap with proposed research model.

Proposed research model

The proposed research model is given in the following chart.

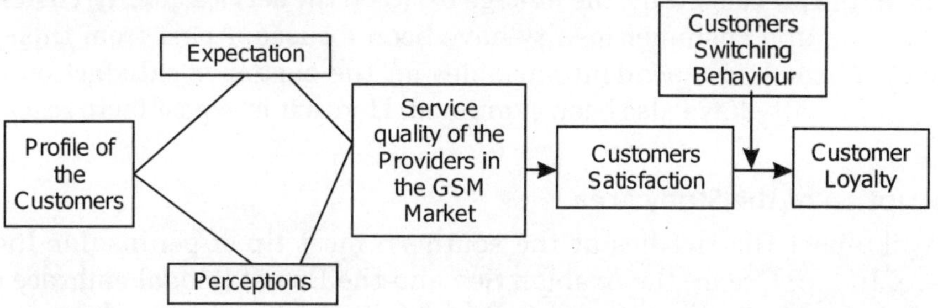

Objectives of the Study

On the basis of the proposed research model, the objectives of the study are confined to:

(*i*) to reveal the profile of the customers in the GSM mobile service market;

(*ii*) to identify the factors influencing to select the service providers;

(*iii*) to evaluate the service quality offered by various service providers;

(*iv*) to examine the service quality gap among the customers;

(*v*) to show the customers satisfaction and its correlates;

(*vi*) to evaluate the impact of service quality on the overall attitude towards the service providers in the GSM market; and

(*vii*) to identify the switching behavior and customer loyalty, its antecedents and consequences in the GSM market.

Research Methodology

Research is defined as a careful investigation or inquiry specially through search for new facts in any branch of knowledge (Dictionary, 1952)[43]. Redman and Moray defined research as "looking for new facts in many branch of knowledge". The research methodology enlightens the methods to be followed in research activities starting from investigation to presentation. Research methodology includes research design, description of the study area, sampling procedure, construct development, framework of analysis and limitation.

Research Design of The Study

"Research design of the arrangement of conditions for collection and analysis of data in a manner that aims to continue relevance to the research purpose with economy in procedure" (Clarie 1962)[44]. In the present study, the expost-facto research design was followed. Singh (1986)[45] has defined expost facto research as a design that draws the influences regarding the relationship between variables on the basis of such independent variables whose manifestations have already occurred. The researcher has no control over the independent variables because they occurred prior to their producing effort. In the present study, the linkage between the service quality, customer satisfaction and customer loyalty have been focused. Apart from this, the impacts of some independent variables on the customer satisfaction and customer loyalty have also been examined. Hence it is expost facto research design.

Description of the Study Area

Kanyakumari District lies at the southern most tip of peninsular India, where, Indian Ocean, the Arabian Sea and the Bay of Bengal embrace one another. By its very location, this District occupies a unique place among the Districts of Tamil Nadu. One of the most important pilgrim centres of India, Kanyakumari is famous for its tourist attractions.

Enjoying comparatively highly rates of rainfall and fertile soils, the District is also called 'Nanjil Nadu', legendary for agricultural productivity. Kanyakumari has a high literacy rate in the State. One can witness the rare scene of the setting of sun and the rising of moon simultaneously on the full moon day at the cape in Kanyakumari.

Location and Demography

The District is situated between 8 8'-8 29' northern longitudes and 76 9-77' eastern longitude, occupying a total area of 1672 sq.km. It is bordered with Thirunelveli District in the North and Northeast, Kerala in the Northwest, Arabian Sea in the West, Indian Ocean in the South, the Gulf of Mannar in the East and Bay of Bengal. It has a coastline of 68 km stretched on the three sides. According to 1991 census, the total population of Kanyakumari District was 16 lakhs. The southern tip of the western ghats tapers off into the District and the torrain is a mix of hills, hilly plains and coastal plains. This small District is famous for its vast green fields, coconut groves, forest wealth and is dotted with a large number of ponds.

History

Kanyakumari has its ancient history dating back to the Sangam age and is a cradle of civilization in this part of India. The District has a large number of historic monuments and temples. Series of kingdoms are known to have ruled Kanyakumari. The most important being the Chera, Chola and Pandy. Up to early fifties of this Century, this region was part of Travancore Samasthanam, present day Kerala, where the Tamil speaking majority population struggled to merge with Tamil Nadu and Kanyakumari became part of Tamil Nadu after the constitution of the State Re-organizing Commission in 1956. On the recommendations of the commission, Agasteeswaram, Thovalai, Kalkulam, Vilavancode and Senkottai taluks were given to Tamil Nadu, among which the first four taluks were grouped to form a new Kanyakumari District. On 1st November 1956, the present Kanyakumari District came into existence with Headquarters at Nagercoil.

Climate

Kanyakumari District has the unique advantage of rainfall during the Southwest and Northeast monsoons. The period of Southwest monsoon is from June to September, while, that of Northeast monsoon is from October to December. Because of its nearness to the equator, its geography and other climate factors, the growth of various food and non-food crops is favoured. Rainfall is generally high in the northern part of the District. The annual rainfall ranges between 90 and 160 cm and the average is 140 cm. The general climate of the District is mild and pleasant for a tropical location. The monsoon winds, the proximity of the sea and the mountains and forests of Western Ghats greatly influence the climate of this District.

Revenue jurisdiction

The District is divided into two revenue Divisions viz., Padmanabhapuram and Nagercoil, having Headquarters at Thuckalay and Nagercoil respectively. There are four Taluks, namely, Vilavancode, Kalkulam, Agasteeswaram and Thovalai. Table 1.1 gives the details of development jurisdiction of the District

Table 1.1: Development Jurisdiction of Kanyakumari District

Sl. No.	Name of the Development Division	Name of the Panchayat Union	Office Location	Area (Sq.Km)
1.	Nagercoil	Agasgteeswaram	Perumalpuram	143.26
		Rajakkamangalam	Pazhavilai	135.49
		Thovalai	Boothapandy	360.91
		Kurunthencode	Kurunthencode	100.54
		Thuckalay	Kozhiporvilai	127.41
		Thiruvattar	Thiruvattar	88.37
2.	Padmanabhapuram	Killiyoor	Tholayavattam	138.86
		Munchirai	Munchirai	71.45
		Melpuram	Pacode	27.57

Source: Records of District Rural Development Department, Nagercoil.

Based on physiography, the District can be divided into three natural Divisions:

1. The north-eastern portion of the Thovalai Taluk constitutes a mountainous Division with spurs from Western Ghats running into it, called high lands.
2. The west and south-west portion of the District is the sea coast which is flat and fairly fertile and called the low lands.
3. Between the mountain range (high lands) and the seacoast (low lands) there exists a strip of undulating valley the midlands with a few streams available for cultivation.

Population

According to 2001 Census, the total population of Kanyakumari District was 23,09,577. The male population is 11,60,562 and the female population is 11,49,015. In this District the rural population is more than the urban population. The density of population is high with 957 per sq.km The total literates in this District are 17,56,754.

The population at various Blocks were shown in the Table 1.2.

Table 1.2: Block wise population detail in Kanniyakumari District

Sl.No.	Blocks	Population
1.	Agasteeswaram	1,97,873
2.	Rajakhamangalam	1,91,305
3.	Thovalai	1,46,919
4.	Kurunthencode	1,46,919
5.	Thuckalay	2,43,578
6.	Thiruvattar	2,39,443
7.	Killiyour	2,42,989
8.	Munchirai	2,64,038
9.	Nagercoil Municipality	2,84,918
10.	Melpuram	2,59,848
11.	Padmanaphapuram	26,429
12.	Colachel	36,625
13.	Kuzhithurai	28,693

Source: District Collectorate, Nagercoil.

Sampling Method

A sample of 4 customers of mobile phone service providers per 10,000 population from each block of the Kanniyakumari District was taken. The total sample size came to 924. Hence the applied sampling technique of the present study is purposive sampling. Out of 924 sampled respondents, the fully responded customers for the interview schedule is 693. Among the 693 customers, the customers of Airtel, Aircel, BSNL, Vodafone, Idea and

Others have been included for the study, since the other service providers are playing a negligible role in the District. Hence, the sample size came to 693 customers.

Construct Development

The present study is classified into three parts for the development of the construct. The first part of the schedule includes the profile of the customers and the factors leading to select the service provider. The second part of the schedule covers the service quality of the service providers and customers satisfaction. The third part of the schedule consists of the switching intention, factors leading to switching and the customer loyalty. A proper care was taken to list out the variables included in each construct at three different parts. The review of previous studies and views of experts had been used to frame the questions in the interview schedule. A pre test was conducted among 50 customers and 50 staff of various service providers. Certain modification, additions and deletions were carried out as per the feed back from the pilot study. The final draft of the schedule was prepared for the data collection.

Framework of Analysis

The statistical analysis has been selected and used to process the collected data according to the requirements of the study. The analysis is selected according to the scale of data and the objectives of the study. The included statistical analysis and its application are presented below:

T-test

The 't' test is one of parametric tests to analyse the significant difference among the two group of samples. It is applied when the criterion variable is in interval scale. The 't' statistics are calculated by

$$t = \frac{\bar{X}_1 - \bar{X}_2}{\frac{(n_1 - 1)\sigma_{s1}^2 (n_2 - 1)\sigma_{s2}^2}{n_1 + n_2 - 2} \times \sqrt{\frac{1}{n_1} + \frac{1}{n_2}}}$$

Which is compared with the degree of freedom of $(n_1 + n_2 - 2)$.

Whereas			
	t	-	't' statistics
	$\bar{X}_1$	-	mean of the first group of sample
	$\bar{X}_1$	-	mean of the second group of sample
	n_1	-	number of samples in the first group
	n_2	-	number of samples in the second group
	σ_{s1}^2	-	variance in the first sample
	σ_{s2}^2	-	variance in the second sample

The 't' test has been applied to test the significant difference among the young and elder customers in GSM market regarding: (*i*) their source of information about the service provider; (*ii*) the variables influencing to choose the service provider; (*iii*) the factors influencing to choose the service provider; (*iv*) the perception on service quality variables and factors; (*v*) the perception on factors leading to the switching behaviour and; (*vi*) the service quality gap.

One way Analysis of Variance (ANVOA)

The one way analysis of variance is applied when the criterion variable is in interval scale and the number of group of samples included for the study is more that two. The 'F' statistics are calculated by

$$F = \frac{Trss/dF}{Ess/dF} = \frac{\text{Greater variance}}{\text{Small variance}}$$

Compared with the F(K-1;N-k) degree of freedom

Whereas F - 'F' statistics

N - Number of sample size

K - Number of groups included

Trss/df - Variance between groups and

Ess/df - Variance within groups.

The one way ANOVA has been administered to examine the association between the profile of customers and their perception on factors leading to choose the service provider, perception and expectation on service quality factors, service quality gaps, factors leading to switching, the overall attitude towards the service provider, and customer loyalty in the market.

Exploratory Factor Analysis (EFA)

The Exploratory factor analysis is used when the researcher wants to narrate the variable into handsome factors and also find the relationship between the variables and narrated factors. It is also called the narration analysis. Whenever the variables related to a particular event are unmanageable or plenty and also in interval scale, the factor analysis has to be executed to narrate these variables into factors. Before applying the factor analysis, the validity of data for factor analysis, the validity of data for factor analysis have to be executed with the help of Kaiser-Mayer-Ohlin (KMO) measure of sampling adequacy and Bartletts test of shpericity. The acceptable KMO measure of sampling adequacy is 0.5, whereas, the acceptable level of significance of chi-square value is up to 0.05 per cent level. In the present study, the factor analysis has been executed to identify the (*a*) factors influencing the choice of their service provider; (*b*) the service quality factors in GSM market; and (*c*) factors leading to their switching behaviours.

Confirmatory Factor Analysis (CFA)

The Confirmatory Factor Analysis has been executed with the help of LISREL 8 software package. It is applied to test the reliability and validity of the variables included in each construct. In the present study, the CFA has been applied to test the reliability and validity of variables in service quality factors, switching factors, overall attitude towards the service provider and the customer loyalty.

Inter correlation matrix

The inter correlation between the factors in a particular construct has been computed for the purpose of testing on the discriminant validity. If the Average Variance Explained (AVE) by the factor is greater than the sum of square correlation between the factor with the other factors, the discriminant validity of the factors is confirmed.

Discriminant Analysis (Two group model)

The discriminant analysis is used when the dependent variable is nominal scale and the independent variable is in interval scale. It is used to identify the important discriminant variables among the two groups formulated in the study. The unstandardized canonical discriminate function was estimated by:

$$Z = a + b_1x_1 + b_2x_2 + b_3x_3 + b_4x_4 +....b_ax_a$$

Whereas

Z = Discriminant criterion

$X_1, X_2,..X_n$ = Discriminant variables

$a_1, b_2..b_a$ = Discriminant coefficients

The Wilk's Lambda was calculated as a multi-variant measure of group difference over discriminating variables. The relative discriminating power of the variables was calculated by:

$$I_j = K_j\left(\bar{X}_{j1} - \bar{X}_{j2}\right)$$

Whereas,

I_j = the important value of jth variable

K_j = unstandardized discriminant co-efficient for the jth variable

X_{jk} = mean of the jth variable for k^{th} group

The relative importance of a variable R_j is given by

$$R_j = \frac{I_j}{\sum_{j=1}^{n} I_j}$$

In the present study, the two group discriminant analysis has been administered to identify the important discriminant factors among the young and elder customers and also the satisfiers and dissatisfiers in the market.

Multiple Regression Analysis

The multiple regression analysis is applied to analyse the impact of independent variables on dependent variable when both the variables are in interval scale. The linear regression model is fitted by:

$$Y = a + b_1x_1 + b_2x_2 + \ldots\ldots\ldots + b_nx_n + 3$$

Whereas Y = Dependent variable

$X_1, X_2 \ldots X_n$ = Independent variables

$b_1, b_2 \ldots b_n$ = Regression coefficient of independent variables

a = intercept and

e = error term

In the present study, the multiple regression analysis has been administered to find out the impact of customer's perception in various service quality factors on their overall attitude towards the mobile phone service offered by the service providers; the impact of switching factors on the switching intention among the customers and the impact of switching factors on the customer loyalty in GSM market.

Structural Equation Modeling (SEM)

The Structural Equation Modeling has been applied with the help of AMOS 5.0 version. In order to analyse the direct, indirect and total effect of independent variables on the dependent variable, the SEM has been administered. In the present study, the included dependent variable is customer loyalty, whereas, the independent variables are the service quality factors. The included mediator variable is overall attitude towards the service provider.

Limitations of the Study

The present study is subjected to the following limitations.

1. The sample size of the study is determined purposively since the number of customers of each service providers in the District is not available.
2. Only the customers of important service providers, namely, Airtel, Aircel, BSNL, Vodafone, Idea and Others have been included for the study, since the other service providers are playing only a minor role in the study area.
3. The variables related to service quality, overall attitude towards service provider, factor loading to switching and customer loyalty have been drawn from the previous studies and the views of experts.
4. The linear relationship between independent and variable has been assumed.
5. The variables related to various construct in the present study are measured at Likert five point scales.

6. The scope of the study is confined to only Kanniyakumari District.
7. The customer loyalty is measured by deterministic approach only (attitude of the customers).

Scheme of the Report

The present study on cellular phone service markets in Kanniyakumari District is presented in seven Chapters.

Chapter I includes the Introduction, Need for the Study, Statement of the Problem, Review of Previous Studies, Proposed Research Model, Objectives of the Study, Methodology of the Study, Limitations and Scheme of the Report.

Chapter II deals with the conceptual framework of the Study.

Chapter III includes the theoretical frame work of the Study. It highlights the cellular phone service market in India, customer base, market share of various service providers and their marketing strategies.

Chapter IV examines the various Profile of the Customers, Source of Information about the service provider, Factors leading to choose the service provider, Association between Profile of Customer and their perception on factors and discriminant factors among the young and elder customers.

Chapter V covers the various service quality factors (SQFs) Level of expectation and perception on SQFs, Service quality gaps, Customer satisfaction on their service providers, Discriminant SQFs among the satisfiers and dissatisfiers; Young and elder customers; and Impact of SQFs on the customers satisfaction.

Chapter VI includes the Switching Behaviours, Factors leading to Switching, Impact of switching factors on switching intentions, Customer loyalty, Impact of switching factors on customer loyalty, Linkage between SQFs, overall attitude and customers' Loyalty.

Chapter VII summarises the Findings, Conclusions, Policy implications and directions for future research.

REFERENCES

1. Reichheld, F.F. and Sasser, W.E. (1990), "Zero defections: Quality Comes to Services", *Harvard Business Review*, September-October, pp. 105-111.
2. 1 Jones, T.O. and Sasser, W.E. (1995), "Why satisfied customer defects?", Harvard Business Review, November-December, pp. 88-99.
3. Fornell, C. and Wernerfelt, B. (1987), "Defensive marketing strategy by customer complaint management: a theoretical analysis", *Journal of Marketing Research*, vol. 24, November, pp. 337-346.
4. Dowling. G.R and Uncles, M., (1997), "Do Customer Loyalty Programs Really Work?", *Sloan Management Review*, Summer, pp. 71082.
5. Rust, R.T. and Zahorit, A.J., (1993), "Customer Satisfaction, Customer Retention, and Market Share", *Journal of Retailing*, 69(2). Summer, pp.193-215.

6. Zeithaml, V.A., Berry, L.L and Parasuraman, A., (1996), "The behavioural Consequences of Service Quality", *Journal of Marketing,* Vol.60, April, pp.31-46.
7. Srikant, A., (2006), "Cellular Mobile Industry in India: A Study", *The ICFAI Journal of Services Marketing,* 4(1), March, pp.34-40.
8. Srivastava, R., Jatin Bhangde, Nivar, Bhatt, Keinal Gogri and Himal Margatia (2006), "Role of Competition in Growing Markets: Telecom Sector", *Indian Journal of Marketing,* 11(3), September, pp.8-16.
9. Revathi, S. and Padmavathy, (2005), "Preferences in Cellular service providers in the post liberalization era", *Indian Journal of Marketing,* February, pp.6-9.
10. Shashikumar Sharma, and D.S. Chauley (2007), "Consumer behaviour towards mobile service providers: An Empirical Study", *The ICFAI Journal of Marketing Management,* 6(1), pp. 41-51.
11. Banumathy, S. and Kalaivani, (2006), "Customers' Attitude Towards Cell Phone Services in Communication System", *Indian Journal of Marketing,* 36 (30, pp. 31-36.
12. Alok Mittal and Prerna Sirohi, (2007), "Factor Affecting, Selection of Cell Services: A Cross-Segmental Study", *Synergy,* 4 (1), January, pp.74-85.
13. Francis Sudhahar, K. and Lydia Nutan, (2005), "An Objective Study of Customer Behaviour in BPL Mobile Cellular Ltd", *Indian Journal of Marketing,* 35(5), May, pp 10-12.
14. Selvaraj, V.M. and Ganesan Malathi, (2005), "A Study of Consumer Behaviour Towards Cell Phone Users in Thuthookudi city", *Indian Journal of Marketing,* May, pp. 23-28.
15. Daxa C. Gohil (2005), "Customers Preferences in Telecom Industry", *Management Trends,* 2(1), October – March, pp.61-68.
16. Vijaykumar, H. and Ruthra Priya, P. (2006), "Satisfaction derived by the Airtel subscribers in Coimbatore", *Indian Journal of Marketing,* 26(10), pp.3-38.
17. Chao, P and Gupta, P.B. (1995), "Information search and Efficiency of consumer choices of New car: Country of origin effects", *International Marketing Review,* 12(6), pp.47-59.
18. Hui, M and Zhou, L. (2002), "Linking Product Evaluations of Purchase intention of country-of-origin effects", *Journal of Global Marketing,* 15(3&4), pp. 95-116.
19. Ahmed, Z., Johnson, J., Ling, C.P., Fang, T.W and Hui, A.K. (2002), "Country-of-origin and Brand effects on consumer's Evaluations of cruise Lines", *International Marketing Review,* 19)2&3), pp.279-302.
20. Essam E.Ibrahim and Pajaree sothornuopatubr (2006), "Country-of-origin and consumer evaluation of mobile Handsets: A comparative study of Scotland and Thailand", *Journal of Consumer Behaviour,* 5(1), pp. 167-196.
21. Balasubramanian, Paterson and Jarvenpaa, S.L. (2000), "Exploring the implications of M-convenience for markets and marketing", *Journal of the Academy of Marketing Science,* 30(3), pp.348-361.
22. Raja, K.G., Uma Sharma and Shashilkala, R., (2006), "Measuring customer satisfaction among mobile Handset End users: AN Empirical Study", *The Icfaian Journal of Management Research,* February, pp. 31-39.
23. Sasikala, P. (2006), "Telecom Services: Measurement of customer satisfaction", *The Icfaian Journal of Management Research,* 5(10), pp.35-53.
24. Chinnadurai, M and Kalpana, B., 92006), "Promotional Strategies of Cellular Services: A Customer Perspective", *Indian Journal of Marketing,* 26(5), pp. 29-37.

25. Yonggui Wang and Hing-Po Lo, (2002), "Service Quality, Customer satisfaction and behaviour intentions", Evidence from Chions Telecommunication Industry", http"// www.emeraldinsight. Com/1463-6697. htm. P.No.: 50-58.

26. Martin Fassnachk and Ibrahim Koese, (2006), "Quality of Electronic Service", *Journal of Services Research,* 9(1), August, pp.19-37.

27. Clement, J. (2005), "Service quality Gap Models: A Re-examination and Extension", *SMART Journal of Business Management Studies,* 1(2), July-December, pp. 87-97.

28. Zillur Rahman (2005), "Service quality: Caps in the Indian Banking Industry", *The ICFAI Journal of Marketing Management,* February, pp. 37-45.

29. Gani, A. and Mushtaq, A. Bhat (2003), "Service quality in Commercial Banks: A Comparati

30. Inger Roos, Bo Edvardsson and Gustafsson (2004), "Customers Switching Patterns in competitive and non-competitive service Industries", *Journal of Service Research,* 6(3), February, pp. 256-271.

31. Yonggui Wang and Hing, Poto (2002), "Service Quality, Customer Satisfaction and Behaviour Intentions", *Journal of Services Marketing,* 4(6), pp.50-60.

32. Anita Seth, Kiran Momaya and Gupta, H.M. (2005), "An Exploratory Investigation of Customer Loyalty and Retention in Cellular Mobile Communication", *Journal of Services Research,* Special Issue, December, pp. 173-185.

33. Bloemer, J., Ruyter, K. and Wetzels, M., (1998), "On the relationship between perceived service quality, service loyalty and switching costs", *International Journal of Industry Management,* 9(5), pp. 436-453.

34. Chada, S.K and Deepa Kapoor (2009), "Effect of Switching Cost, Service Quality and Customer Satisfaction on Customer Loyalty of Cellular Service Providers in Indian Market", *The ICFAI University Journal of Marketing Management,* 8(1), pp. 23-37.

35. Gerpost, T.J., Rams, W and Shindler, A. (2001), "Customer retention, loyalty and satisfaction in the German mobile cellular telecommunication market", Telecommunication policy, 25(4), pp. 249-269.

36. Lee, J. Lee, and Feick, L. (2001), "The impact of switching costs on the customer satisfaction – loyalty link: Mobile phone service in France", *Journal of services marketing,* 15(1), pp. 35-48.

37. Wang, Y and Lo, H. (2002), "Service Quality, Customer Satisfaction and Behavioural Intentions-Evidence from Chinas' Telecommunications Industry", *The Journal of Policy, Regulation and Strategy for Telecommunication Information and Media,* 4(6), pp.50-60.

38. Rana Weera, C and Neely, A. (2003), "Some moderating effects on the Service Quality–Customer Retention Link", *International Journal of Operations and Production Management,* 23(2), pp. 230-248.

39. Kim, M., Park, M, and Jeong, D. (2004), "The effects of customer satisfaction and snitching barriers on customer loyalty in Korean mobile Telecommunication Services", *Telecommunication Policy*, 28(2), pp. 145-159.

40. Palkar Apoorva, (2004), "Determinants of customer satisfaction for Cellular Service Providers", *Udyaog Pragati*, 28(1), January-March, pp.19-26.

41. Ray Subhasis and Sarkar Avishek (2006), "Analysing influence of Brand Vis-à-vis. Price in Indian Mobile industry", *The ICFAI Journal of Marketing Management*, 5(4), pp. 46-57.
42. Selvarasu, A. Gomathi Shankar, K. and Loganathan, (2006), "GSM Mobile Service in Telecom Sector: An Ontology of Quality of Service", *The ICFAI Journal of Service Marketing*, 4(4), pp. 36-44.
43. The Advanced Learner's Dictionary of current English, Oxford, 1952, p. 1069.
44. Clarie Selltiz and others, (1962), "Research methods in Social Sciences, p.50.
45. Singh, S. (1986), *Statistical Techniques in Agricultural Research*, Oxford and IBH Publishing Co., New Delhi, pp. 308-30.

2 Conceptual Frame Work

Introduction

The various concepts used in the present study are derived from various previous studies. Cellular operators create a revolution in the life of people. It gives an opportunity to reach people and be reachable at all times.

Concepts

In this part of the Thesis, the researcher has provided various concepts which are derived from various previous Studies related to the present Topic.

Factors influencing Selection of Cellular Services

The factors influencing the selection of cellular services represent the number of factors, which directly or indirectly influence the customers to select a particular cellular service (Nautiyal Jyoti, 1999)[1]. The factors influencing the choice of the cellular services are higher number of included minutes, best voice clarity, pulse of shorter duration, additional feature, no extra charge, multimedia messaging, low administrative changes, least number of call drops, call waiting facility, call conferencing facility, good storage capacity in SIM, call recording facility, reasonable charges for outgoing calls, least number of formalities, large number of promotional schemes, prepaid or post paid facility, low cast SIM and others (Agarwal Pradeep, 1999)[2]. In the present Study, the variables influencing the choice of a particular cell phone service are identified as twenty seven. They are presented in Table 2.1.

Table 2.1: Variables influencing to Select Cellular Services

Sl.No.	Variables
1.	Free incoming facility
2.	Nominal charges on calls
3.	Network coverage
4.	Free SMS facility
5.	Frequent Schemes
6.	Voice Clarity
7.	Prepaid/Post paid facility
8.	Low Cost SIM Card
9.	Brand Image
10.	Call waiting facility
11.	Large number of promotional schemes
12.	Inter-Network coverage
13.	Low activation charges
14.	Multi-media messaging facility
15.	Goodwill of the provider
16.	Natural Roaming facility
17.	Minimum security amount
18.	Lesser office formalities
19.	Positive words of mouth
20.	Increased validity period
21.	Higher Numbers included
22.	Special/festival offer
23.	Reasonable charges on outgoing calls
24.	Classification of peak and off peak hours
25.	Good in house coverage
26.	Multi-National Company
27.	Itemised Billing

The customers are asked to rate these variables at five point scale.

Service quality perceptions

The delivery of a service has been described as a 'performance' featuring the service provider and the customer (Bitner, 1992)[3]. It is during this performance that the actions and behaviour of service employees become the crucial determinants of service quality as perceived by consumers (Hartline and Ferrell, 1996)[4]. The perception on service quality is measured by the instrument developed by Parasuraman *et al.,* (1988)[5]. It is the SERVQAUL scale. It examines the perceived gap between the customer's expectations of the service quality (Crowin and Taylor, 1992[6], Peter *et al.*, 1993[7], and Bebko, 2004[8]). SERVPERF is measurement of the customer's perception of the performance of the service providers. In the present Study, the SERVPERF scale is used to measure the service quality in mobile phone service industry.

Service researches have suggested that the search for universal conceptualization of the service quality construct may be fertile (Levitt, 1981[9], Lovelock, 1983)[10] and arguments have been advanced to suggest that service quality is either or context specific (Babakus and Boller, 1992)[11]. Thus to be of practical utility, a service construct should not only be operational (non-global), but also context specific. The identification of service quality variables in the mobile phone service industry is based on Lapierre's (1996)[12] observation:

(*i*) Service quality research is critically dependent on the quality of the operational measures;

(*ii*) Given the nature of service, the search for universal conceptualization of service quality may be fertile; and

(*iii*) Construct areas of important for the examination of substantive relationships.

The service quality variables in mobile telecommunications are identified from the reviews (Holbrook, 1994[13] Dabholkar *et al.,* 2000;[14] Wang *et al.,* 2002)[15]. In total, there are 31 variables which have been included for the analysis. These are presented in Table 2.2.

Table 2.2: Variables in service quality of the service provider in GSM market

Sl.No.	Variables in Service Quality
1	2
1.	Providing service as promised
2.	Connecting call easily
3.	Telling customer exactly what services will be performed
4.	Employees still confidence in customers
5.	Speedy delivery of SMS
6.	Getting news, Jobs and others
7.	Electronic recharging
8.	Sincere in solving the problem
9.	Facility of getting missed call
10.	Recharging without hassles through easy deal
11.	Providing prompt service to customers
12.	Getting booster exchange
13.	Performing service right at the first time

1	2
14.	Easy recharging
15.	Neat and knowledgeable employees
16.	Various options in recharging coupons
17.	Immediate Customer care
18.	No problems in setting calls
19.	Providing service at the promised time
20.	Recharge facilities
21.	Customers feel comfortable interacting with employees
22.	Song options for dialer times
23.	Modernization of networks
24.	Voice clarity Net works
25.	Employees are consistent
26.	Quick activation of number
27.	Frequent scheme
28.	Maintain error-free-records
29.	Employees are trust worthy
30.	Willing to help customers
31.	Always ready to respond to customers request

The customers are asked to rate these service quality variables at five point scale regarding their level of perception and expectation on these.

Service Quality Gap

The service quality gap results from a comparison of expectations and perceptions (Parasuraman, *et al.,* 1998)[16]. The service quality gap is measured by a scale, namely, SERVQUAL scale. The foundation for the SERVQUAL scale is the gap model proposed by Parasuraman *et al.,* (1985)[17]. The SERVQUAL scale is supported by Carman (1990)[18], Finn and Lamb (1991)[19] and Spreng and Singh (1993). In an equation form, their operationalization of service quality can be expressed as follows:

$$SQ_i = \sum_{j=1}^{k} \left(P_{ij} - E_{ij}\right)$$

Whereas

SQ_i – perceived service quality of individual 'i'

k – number of service attributes / items

p – perception of individual 'i' with respect to performance of a service firm attribute 'j'

E – service quality expectation for attribute 'j' that is the relevant norm for individual 'i'

In the present Study, the service quality gap is measured by using the SERVQUAL scale.

Customers Satisfaction

Customer satisfaction has long been recognized in marketing thought and practice as a central concept as well as an important goal of all business activities (Anderson[20] *et al.,* 1994; Yi, 1990[21]). Consumer satisfaction has different level of specificity in various studies. Although satisfaction with, say, a product attribute (Beltman, 1974)[22], a sales person (Swan and Oliver, 1985)[23], and a consumption experience (Beardenand Teel, 1983)[24] may be useful, a more fundamental level is and should be the satisfaction with a product commodity or service.

Rust and Oliver (1994)[25] defined satisfaction as the "customer's fulfillment response", which is an evaluation as well as an emotion-based response to a service. Cronin *et al.,* (2000)[26] assessed service satisfaction using items that include interest, enjoyment, surprise, anger, wise choice and doing the right thing. In the present Study, the customer satisfaction on the mobile phone service is measured at five point scale. In the present Study, there are eleven variables included to measure overall attitude towards the service provider. These are given in Table 2.3.

Table 2.3: Variables related Customers Satisfaction towards the Service Providers

Sl. No.	Variables
1.	Activation formalities
2.	Call charges
3.	Plan options
4.	Clarity of signals
5.	Service quality
6.	Product quality
7.	Connectivity
8.	Basic services
9.	Value added services
10.	Coverage of Network
11.	Voice clarity

Customer switching behaviour

Customers in the telecommunication industry, most often, only partly switch their telecommunication services to a competitor (Edvardsson *et al.,* 2002)[27]. The reasons for switching referred to here, have been related to the particular kinds of switching described as total, partial or internal according to a unique pattern of customer preferences, with behaviour as the reference point.

This pattern indicates the industry specific configuration of reasons for consumer sensitiveness to switching (Roos, 2002[28]). The switching determinants are: Influential trigger-price partial change Situational trigger–Ranger of Goods– Partial Change and Reactional Trigger–Service Policy–Total Change (Johnson and Gustafsson, 2000[29] and Johnson, 2001[30]).

Customer Switching represents the switch either total or partly to another service provider (Edvardson and Roos, 2003[31], Roos Innger, 1999[32]). The switching intention among the customers may be caused by situational trigger, influential bigger and reactional trigger. (Roos, 2002[33], Bolton and Lemon, 1999[34]). The switching configurations in telecommunication industries are price, customer support, change in product use and systems failure (Ganesh *et al.*, 2000[35], Sirdeshmukh *et al.*, 2002[36]). The reasons for switching behaviour and intentions among the customers in mobile phone service industries are identified with the help of the above-said reviews. There are 25 variables identified as the reasons for switching in the present Study. These are given in Table 2.4.

Table 2.4: Variables Leading to Switching

Sl.No.	Variables
1.	Network
2.	Free incoming
3.	Coverage
4.	Fxcellent service
5.	Tariff
6.	Security deposits
7.	Connectivity
8.	Attractive plans
9.	Government cellular service
10.	Lesser switching cost
11.	New operator brings less cost
12.	New operator delivery expected service
13.	Better new recharge cost
14.	Innovative ideas
15.	Frequent offer
16.	Value added service
17.	Friends and relatives
18.	Popularity in the market
19.	Multi-usage
20.	Discount
21.	Free calls
22.	Lesser subscription cost
23.	Extra benefits drawn from new operators
24.	Low premature termination of calls
25.	Comparative advantage

The customers are asked to rate these 25 variables at five point scale according to the order of importance.

Customer Loyalty

Customer loyalty refers to a favourate attitude towards a particular brand in addition to purchasing it repeatedly (Day, 1969)[37]. It is a relationship between relative attitudes towards an entity and repeat patronage behaviour (Dick and Rasu, 1994)[38]. It is a situation when repeat purchase behaviour is accompanied by a psychological bond; and repeat purchase intentions and behaviours (Cronin and Taylor, 1992)[39]. Customers loyalty sometimes has been operationalised as a behavioural measure and at other times as an attitude. Behavioural measures include probability of purchase (Farley, 1964)[40], purchase frequency (Brody and Cunningham, 1968)[41], repeat purchase behaviour (Brown, 1952)[42], purchase sequence and multiple aspects of purchase behaviour.

Attitudinal approaches are focussed mainly brand recommendations (Boulding *et al.,* 1993)[43], resistance to superior products (Narayandas, 1996)[44], Willingness to pay a price premium. (Zeithammal *et al.,* 1996)[45] and repurchase intention (Anderson and Sullivan, 1992)[46]. In the present Study, the customer loyalty in mobile telecommunication market has been measured with the help of 10 variables. These are presented in Table 2.5.

Table 2.5: Variables in Customer Loyalty

Sl.No.	Variables
1.	Continue with current service provider
2.	Wish to have one more connection
3.	Pride of my service provider
4.	Recommend my service provider to others
5.	Higher trust on my service provider
6.	Inclination to buy other services
7.	Lesser price sensitive
8.	Service differentiation from my service provider
9.	Competitive advantage my service provider
10.	No other alternative to my service provider.

The customers are asked to rate the above - said 10 variables at five point scale according to their order of importance attached herewith.

REFERENCES

1. Nautiyal Jyoti (1999), "A study on consumer perception of service quality with special reference to RPG cell com and Reliance Telecom", Unpublished Major Project Report, PIMR, Indore.
2. Agarwal Pradeep (1999), "Comparison of customer satisfaction level of RPG and Reliance Telecom customers", Unpublished major Project Report, PIMR, Indore.

3. Bitner, M.J. (1992), "Service Capes: The Impact of Physical Surroundings on Customers and Employees", *Journal of Marketing,* 56(April), pp.57-71.
4. Hartline, M.D. and Ferrell, O.C. (1996), "The Management of Customer Contact Service Employees: An Empirical Investigation", *Journal of Marketing*, 60(4), pp. 52 – 61.
5. Parasuraman, A., Zathanl, V.A and beny, L.L. (1988), "SERVQUAL: A Multiple Item Scale for Measuring Consumer Receptions of Service Quality", *Journal of Retailing*, 64 (Spring) pp. 12 – 40.
6. Crowin, J.J. and Taylor, S.A. (1992), "Measuring Service Quality: are Examination and Extension", *Journal of Marketing*, 56(3), pp. 55 – 68.
7. Peter, J., Churchill, G and Brown, T (1993), "Caution in the use of Difference Sores in Consumer Research", *Journal of consumer Research*, 19(4), pp.655–662.
8. Bebko, C.P (2000), "Service Intangibility and its Impact on Consumer Expectations of Service Quality", *Journal of Services Marketing*, 14(1), pp.9- 26.
9. Levilt, T. (1981), "Marketing intangible products and product intangibles", *Harvard Business Reviews*, 59(3), pp. 94 – 102.
10. Lovelock, C.H. (1983), "Classifying Services to gain Strategic Marketing Insights", *Journal of Marketing*, 47(3), pp. 9 – 20.
11. Babakus and Roller, G.W(1992), "An empirical assessment of the SERVQUAL scale", *Journal of Business Research*, 24(3), pp.253 – 68.
12. Lapierre, J. (1996), "Service quality: the construct, the dimensionality, and its measurement", in swartz, T.A., Bower, D.E and Brown, S.W (eds), Advances in services marketing and management, Vol. 5, JAI press Juc., Greenwich, CT, pp. 45 – 70.
13. Hulbrook, M.B. (1994), "The nature of customer value: an axiolosy of services in the consumption experience", in Rusk, R.T and Oliver, R.L (Eds), service: new directions in Theory and practice, Sage Publications, Inc, Thousand Oaks, C.A, pp.21-71.
14. Dabholhan, P.A, Shepered C.D and Thorpe, D.I. (200), "A comprehensive Frame Work for Service Quality: and Investigation of Critical Conceptual Measurement issues though a Longitudinal Study", *Journal of Retailing*, 76 (2), pp. 139 – 173.
15. Wong, Y, H.P., Hui, Y.V. and Char, M. (2002), "The antecedents and consequences of service quality and product quality revisited: evidence from telecom industry in china", in quality in service: crossing borders, University of Vichima, Canada, pp.131–141.
16. Parasuraman, A., Zeithammal, V.A. and Berry, L.L. (1988), "SERVQUAL: A multiple item scale for measuring consumer perceptions of service quality", *Journal of Retailing,* 64(1), pp.12-40..
17. Parasuraman, A., Zeithammal, V.A., and Berry, L.L. (1988), "A conceptual model of service quality and its implications for future research", *Journal of Marketing,* 49 (Fall), pp.41-50.
18. Carman, J.M., (1990), "Consumer Perceptions of Service quality: An Assessment of SERVQUAL Dimensions", *Journal of Retailing*, 66(1), pp.33-35..
19. Finn, D.W. and Lamb, C.W., (1991), "An Evaluation of the SERVQUAL scale in a retailing setting", in Holman, R. and Solomon, M.R., (edr.), Advances in Consumer Research, Provo, UTI., Association for consumer researcher, pp.480-493.
20. Anderson, E.W., Fornell, C. and Leomann, D.R., (1994), "Customer Satisfaction, Market Share and Profitability: Findings from Sweden", *Journal of Marketing*, 58 (3), pp.53-66.

21. Yi, Y., (1990), "A Critical View of Consumer Satisfaction", in Zeithmal, V.A., (Eds.), *Review of Marketing*, 1990, American Marketing Association, Chicago, IC, pp.68-123.

22. Beltman, J.R., (1974), "A others hold model of attribute satisfaction decision", *Journal of Consumer Research*, Vol.1, September, pp.30-35.

23. Swan, J.E. and Oliver, R.L., (1985), "Automobile buyer satisfaction with the sales person related to equity and disconfirmation", in Hunt, H.K. and Day, R.L., (Eds.), Consumer Satisfaction, Disconfirmation and Complaining Behaviour, Indiana University Press, Blommington, IN.

24. Bearden, W.O. and Teel, J.E., (1983), "Selected Determinants of Consumer satisfaction and complaint reports", *Journal of Marketing Research*, Vol.20, February, pp.21-28.

25. Rust, R.T., and Oliver, R.L. (1994), "Service Quality: Insights and Managerial Implications from the Frontier", in Rust, R.T. and Oliver, R.L., (Eds.) Service Quality: New Directions in Theory and Practice, Sage Publications, Thousand Oaks, CA, pp.72-94.

26. Cronin, J.J., Brady, M.K. and Hult, T.M. (2000), "Assessing the effects of quality, value, consumer satisfaction on consumer behavioural intentions in service environment", *Journal of Retailing*, 76 (2), pp.193-216.

27. Edvardsson, Gustagsson, and Inver Ross (2002), "Comparing Switching patterns in competitive and non-competitive markets", 11th Annual American Marketing Association Frontiers in Service Conference, June 27-29, Maastrucht, The Netherlands.

28. Roos, Inger (2002), "Methods of Investigating Critical Incidents: A Comparative Review", *Journal of Services Research*, 4(3), pp.193-204.

29. Johnson and Anders Gustafasson (2000), "Improving Customer Satisfaction, Loyalty and Profit, An Integrated Measurement and Measurement System", San Francisco: Jossey - Bass.

30. Johnson, D. (2001), "Customer Switching Behaviour in on line services: An Exploratory Story", *Journal of the Academy of Marketing Science*, 29(4), pp.374-390.

31. Evardson, B.O., and Innger Roos, (2003), "Customer Complaints and Switching Behaviour–A Study of Relationship Dynamics in a Telecommunication Company", *Journal of Relationship Marketing*, 2(1/2), pp. 43-68.

32. Roos, Inger (1999), "Switching Processes in Customer Relations", *Journal of Services Research*, 2(1), pp.68-85.

33. Roos, Inger (2002), "Methods of Investigating Critical Incidents: A Comparative Review", *Journal of Service Research,* 4(3), pp.193-204.

34. Bolton Ruth, N. and N. Lemon (1999), "A Dynamic Model of Customers Usage of Services: Usage as an Antecedent and Consequence of Satisfaction", *Journal of Marketing Research*, 36(3), pp.171-186.

35. Ganesh, J., Arnold, J., and Kristy, E., (2000), "Understanding the Customer base of service providers: An Examination of the differences between Switches and Stayers", *Journal of Marketing*, 64(3), pp.65-87.

36. Srideshmukh, Jagdip Singh and Barry Sabol (2002), "Consumer Trust, Value and Loyalty in Relational Exchanges", *Journal of Marketing*, 66(January), pp. 15-37.

37. Day, G.S., (1969), "A Two-Dimensional Concept of brand loyalty", *Journal of Advertising Research*, 9(3), pp. 29-36.
38. Dick, S.A., and Basu, K. (1994), "Customer Loyalty: Toward and Integrated Conceptual framework", *Journal of the Academy of Marketing Science*, 22(2), pp. 99-113.
39. Cronin, J.J. and Taylor, S.A. (1992), "Measuring service quality: a re-examination and extension", *Journal of Marketing*, 58 (2), pp.125-131.
40. Farely, J.V. (1964), "Why Does Brand Loyalty vary over products?", *Journal of Marketing Research*, 1 (4), pp.9-14.
41. Brody, R.P., and Cunningham, S.M. (1968), "Personality variables and consumer decision process", *Journal of Marketing Research*, 5 (1), pp.50-57.
42. Brown, G.H. (1952), "Brand Loyalty-Fact or Fiction?", Advertising Age, 23 (1), pp. 53-55.
43. Boulding W.K alva, Staelin R. and Zeithaml, V.A. (1993), "A Dynamic Process Model of Service Quality : from expectations to behavioural intentions", *Journal of Marketing Research*, Vol.30, February, pp. 7-27.
44. Narayandas, N., (1996), "The Link between customer satisfaction and customer loyalty: An Empirical Investigation", Working Paper No.97-017, Harvard Business School, Boston, MA.
45. Zeithaml, V.A., Berry, L.L. and Parasuraman, A., (1996), "The behavioural consequences of service quality", *Journal of Marketing*, Vol. 60, pp. 31-46.
46. Anderson, E.W. and Sullivan, V.W. (1993), "The Antecedents and consequences of customer satisfaction for firms", *Marketing Science*, 12 (2), pp. 125-143.

Theoretical Frame Work of the Study

Introduction

Competition in the Telecom Sector, coupled with the provision of inter connection has widened consumers' choice. These changes have also posed a challenge to evaluate the demand relations in the case of new products and services, such as, mobile and wireless telephony. In this Chapter the researcher has presented a detailed note on the Cellular Telephone Industry in the Country.

World-mobile Cellular Subscribers

The number of mobile subscriber, world wide, is proliferating. The world wide mobile cellular subscribers from 1995 to 2008 are presented in Table 3.1.

Table 3.1: World–mobile Cellular Subscribers (Millions) (1995-2008)

Sl. No.	Year	Subscribers	Annual Growth
1.	1995	91	62.50
2.	1996	145	59.34
3.	1997	215	48.28
4.	1998	318	47.91
5.	1999	490	54.09
6.	2000	740	51.02
7.	2001	955	29.05
8.	2002	1166	22.09
9.	2003	1414	21.27
10.	2004	1758	24.33
11.	2005	2086	18.66
12.	2006	2569	23.15
13.	2007	2937	14.32
14.	2008	3607	22.81

Source: International Telecommunication Union, Yearbook of Statistics 2008)

It is seen from Table 3.1 that the number of subscribers in mobile cellular service market has increased from 91 millions in 1995 to 3607 millions in 2008. The higher annual growth rate of subscribers has been identified as 62.50 and 59.34 in 1995 and 1996 respectively. The annual growth rates of subscribers base in 2007 and 2008 are 14.32 and 22.81 respectively.

Telecom Industry in India

India describes the fifth largest Telecom Network in the world and the second largest amongst the developing economies, after China, with an annual growth rate of 22 per cent in basic telephones and over 100 per cent in cellular phones and internet services[1]. This remarkable growth in the telecom sector has been possible only after the adoption of liberalization policy when the telecom sector was thrown open for competition by allowing private participation. Prior to liberalization, the Government-owned Department of Telecommunications (DOT) enjoyed the monopoly position. Moreover, the only service offered by DOT was that of fixed lines. This was characterized by under investment, outdated equipment, services that were not customer-centric and growth well below the potential of the market (Jain, 2001). This was reflected in sluggish growth of the Telecom Sector.

Telecommunication is one of the most vital of all the infrastructure services today. It is not only essential for the growth and development of every other sector of the economy, but also for the integration of Indian Economy with the rest of the world. Today, call rates in India are among the cheapest in the world. The total number of telephones rose from just 22.8 million in 1999 to 101.8 million in May 2005. The next milestone for this Industry is to cross the 250 million telephone mark by 2007, along with reaching a tele-density of 22 per cent. The current tele-density of India is 9 per cent, as against 55 per cent in China and over 100 per cent in the US, Germany and Japan.

The expansion of the telecom industry in India has been fuelled by a massive growth in mobile phone users which had reached a level of 46 million users in November 2004. This exponential growth of mobile telephony can be attributed to the introduction of digital cellular technology and decrease in tariffs due to competitive pressure. For the first time in India in November 2004, the total number of cellular subscribers' base had exceeded the fixed line subscribers' base. India offers an unprecedented opportunity for telecom service operators, infrastructure vendors, manufacturers and associated services companies. A host of factors are contributing to enlarged opportunities for growth investment in Telecom. They are:

(*i*) an expanding Indian Economy with increased focus on the services sector.

(*ii*) population mix moving favourably to younger age profile.

(*iii*) urbanization with increasing income.

Investors can look to capture the gains of the Indian Telecom boom and diversify their operations outside developed economies that are marked by saturated telecom markets and lower GDP growth rates. With most of the regulatory uncertainty getting over, there is heightened interest in Indian Telecom.

The Telecom Industry is considered as having the highest potential for investment in India. Recognizing that the Telecom Sector is one of the prime movers of the Economy, the Governments, regulatory and policy initiatives have also been directed towards establishing a world class telecommunications infrastructure in India.

Performance of Telecom Sector

Two district phases can be noted in the development of Telecom Sector. The first phase is prior to liberalization, which is associated with sluggish growth in this Sector. The second phase began with the adoption of liberalization policy. In the second phase, the Telecom Sector experienced remarkable development. In order to examine the performance of telecom sector, one has to study the pattern of change in different indicators of Telecom Sector. Tele density, amount of investment in telecom sector, amount of revenue generated in the Telecom Sector, number of players, usage, waiting lists, fault correction rates and technology are good indicators of studying the development of Telecom Sector. The study evaluates the status of these indicators prior to liberalization and after the adoption of the policy of liberalization. Table 3.2 explains the details of Telecom indicators in the pre-liberalization and post-liberalization periods.

As shown in Table 3.2 the teledensity was negligible prior to liberalization. In the year 1990, the teledensity was 0.59 and it rose to 1.29 in the year 1995. It further rose to 3.55 in the year 2000. As far the latest figures are available for the Study, the teledensity was 7.10 in 2003. These figures clearly show that the teledensity has improved tremendously after the introduction of economic reforms.

Interesting changes are observed in the National Long Distance (NLD) calls. The data presented in Table 3.3 reveals that NLD calls have declined particularly after 1995. The number of NLD calls increased till 1990 and it numbers to 24 million. But, thereafter, NLD calls have started declining. The reasons for this decline could be attributed to the introduction of mobile telephony and expansion of other means of communications.

It is possible to find convincing explanations for the decline in NLD calls after 1995. In the year 1995, mobile telephony was introduced and other means of quicker communications were also penetrating into the market. Soon after liberalization, the monopoly of BSNL suffered a major set back with the addition of one more player in the Telecom Sector. An element of stiff competition was further introduced when the number of

Table 3.2: Telecom Indicators in the pre-liberalization and Post-liberalization Period

Sl. No.	Year	Teledensity	Annual Telecom Investment	Annual Telecom Revenue	Waiting List	Faults Per 100 Main Lines	NLD Calls	ILD Minutes	Cell Phone Users
1.	1960	0.075145	-	-	189415	-	-	-	-
2.	1965	0.125898	2.37E+08	6.74E+08	294557	-	58150000	-	-
3.	1970	0.176849	5.54E+08	1.42E+09	414368	-	85900000	-	-
4.	1975	0.236090	1.75E+09	3.15E+09	637100	-	1.34E+08	2378310	-
5.	1980	0.312035	2.59E+09	6.58E+09	446505	-	1.69E+08	8486000	-
6.	1985	0.414906	8.51E+09	1.31E+10	976155	382.8	2.18E_08	26733000	-
7.	1990	0.599638	2.77E+10	4.57E+10	1960997	222.0	2.24E+08	1.47E+08	-
8.	1995	1.299472	8.22E+10	1.34E+11	2277000	195.6	76400000	3.42E_08	76680
9.	2000	3.557228	1.58E+11	3.2E+11	2916720	165.5	3370000	5.4E+08	357709
10.	2001	4.378485	1.66E+11	3.61E+11	1648845	150.0	-	5.48E+08	6431520
11.	2002	4.378485	-	3.87E+11	-	126.0	-	6.6E+08	12687637
12.	2003	7.103042	-	-	-	-	-	-	26154404

Source: World Telecommunication Indicators, Database, International Telecommunication Union (ITU), Geneva.

service providers in the market rose to four. Today in the fag end of 2004, the total number of telecom service providers is 12.

Mile Stones in Telecom Sector of India

The Indian Telecom Sector crossed several milestones in its history. The important milestones especially from 1991 are illustrated in Table 3.3.

Table 3.3: Telecom Sector Milestones

Sl. No.	Year	Event
1.	1991	National Telecom Policy formed, telecom equipment sector liberalized
2.	1992	Value added services like paging and very small aperture terminals (VSATs) opened to private sector, foreign investment guidelines initiated
3.	1994	Guidelines for private sector participation in basic services and cellular services
4.	1996	First round cellular services and basic services launched
5.	1997	Telecom Regulatory Authority of India formed
6.	1998	Internet service providers' policy announced, second round of bids completed
7.	1999	New Telecom policy, migration form license fees to revenue sharing
8.	2000	National long distance opened, long distance tariffs reduced, DOT corporatized
9.	2001	Fourth round of basic service licenses and cellular licenses finalized
10.	2002	International long distance opened up to private sector

It is clear from Tables 3.3 that the Telecom Sector has been on the path of development of the Country.

Telecom Statistics in India

The telecom statistics in India are subjected to vast growth and development especially after globalization. The total subscribers, teledensity, fixed line, addition and mobile in Indian telecom industry during March, 2008, April, 2008, and May 2008 are shown in Table 3.4.

From the Table 3.4, it is inferred that the total subscribers have increased from 150.53 millions during March 2008 to 156.04 millions during May 2008. The tele density has also increased from 11.42 to 12.53 during the same period. The fixed line is increasing from 50.68 millions to 51.92 lines during the same period. The additions during the month of March, April and May are 0.58, 0.66 and 0.73 millions respectively. The mobile services have been increasing from 63.08 millions during March 2008 to 68.14 millions during May 2008.

Table 3.4: Telecom Statistics

Sl.No.	Particulars	March 2008	April 2008	May 2008
1.	Total subscribers (in million)	150.53	152.04	156.04
2.	Tele Density	11.42	12.03	12.53
3.	Fixed line (in millions)	50.68	51.63	51.92
4.	Additions during the month (in millions)	0.58	0.66	0.73
5.	Mobile (in millions)	63.08	65.77	68.14

Source: www. Dotindia.com

From April 1991 to March 2003 the total Foreign Direct Investment (FDI) in Telecom was '9590.7 cr. The cellular industry had a phenomenal growth rate of 91.8 per cent per annum from July 1999 to July 2003. The increase in subscriber bases is due to genuine demand in the market arising out of an increased need for mobility and the increasing affordability of cellular services. The cellular industry had a major positive impact on the Economy and the lifestyle of people. The Global System for Mobile Technology (GSM) subscriber reached 17.4 million in August 2003. Cellular operators have benefited by the addition of long distance revenue to their service, which is a big market and has a tremendous growth potential. Some of the major Companies in the cellular mobile segment include Bharti, Reliance, BSNL, Hutch and Idea.

Mobile Subscribers in India

Mobile phones and fixed line phones are good substitutes and therefore, the entry of mobile phones in 1995 started competing with the fixed line phones. At the time of entry of mobile phones into the market, the call rates were as high as '12 per minute in the year 1996, which came down to '8 per minute in the year 2000. A substantial reduction in intracircle, intercircle, and international call rates is observed on a regular basis during these ten years after the entry of mobile phones into the market. An interesting trend is observed after the entry of mobile phones into the market. The total number of fixed line users started declining whereas, the total number of mobile users showed an increasing trend. In cities the mobile phones have outnumbered fixed lines since long. This trend has also started penetrating into big cities. The increase in mobile subscribers vis-à-vis fixed line subscribers is shown in Table 3.5.

Table 3.6 explains that the mobile phone service subscribers as percentage of basic subscribers in India. It is increasing from 10.94 per cent in 2000-01 to 92.45 per cent in 2007-08. It shows the fast growth of mobile phone service subscribers providers in India.

Table 3.5: Mobile Substances as Percentage of Basic Subscriptions India (2001-2008)

Year	2000-01	2001-02	2002-03	2003-04	2004-05	2005-06	2006-07	2007-08
Percentage	10.94	16.73	30.58	78.70	81.45	86.36	90.08	92.45

Source: www.dot.india.com.

CELLULAR SERVICE PROVIDERS IN INDIA

Apart from BSNL, there are so many important service providers that who are playing important role in Indian mobile phone service market. The service provider, its regions and the number of telecom circles in each service provider is illustrated in Table 3.6.

Table 3.6: Cellular Service Providers and the Technology Used

Sl. No.	Service Provider	Region	Number of Telecom Circles	Technology Used
1	2	3	4	5
1.	BSNL	Chennai, Kolkatta, Maharashtra, Gujarat, Andhra Pradesh, Karnataka, TamilNadu, Kerala, Punjab, Haryana, West Uttar Pradesh, East, Uttar Pradesh, Rajasthan, Madhya Pradesh, West Bengal, Himachal Pradesh, Bihar, Orissa, Assam, Nepal, Jammu and Kashmir	21	GSM & CDMA
2.	Bharti	Delhi, Mumbai, Chennai, Kolkata, Maharashtra, Gujarat, Tamil Nadu, Andhra Pradesh, Karnataka, Kerala, Punjab, Haryana, West Uttar Pradesh, East Uttar Pradesh, Rajasthan Orissa, Madhya Pradesh, West Bengal, Himachal Pradesh, Jammu and Kashmir.	20	GSM
3.	Reliance	Delhi, Kolkata, Mumbai, Chennai, Maharashtra, Gujarat, Andhra Pradesh, Karnataka, Tamil Nadu, Kerala, Punjab, Haryana, West Uttar Pradesh, East Uttar Pradesh, Rajasthan, Orissa, Bihar, Assam, Madhya Pradesh West Bengal, Himachal Pradesh, Nepal	22	GSM & CDMA
4.	Hutch	Delhi, Mumbai, Chennai, Kolkata, Gujarat, Andhra Pradesh, Karnataka, Punjab, Haryana, West Uttar Pradesh, East Uttar Pradesh, Rajasthan, West Bengal	13	GSM
5.	Idea	Delhi, Maharashtra, Gujarat, Andhra Pradesh, Karnataka, Haryana, West Uttar Pradesh, Madhya Pradesh	8	

1	2	3	4	5
6.	Tata Teleservices	Delhi, Mimbai, Chennai, Maharashtra, Gujarat, Andhra Pradesh, Karnataka, Tamil Nadu, Rajasthan, Bihar, Orissa	11	
7.	BPL Mobile	Mumbai, Maharashtra, Tamil Nadu, Kerala	4	
8.	Aircel Cellular	Chennai, Tamil Nadu	2	
9.	MTNL	Delhi, Mumbai	2	
10.	Space Communications	Karnataka, Punjab	2	
11.	HFCL	Punjab	1	
12.	Shyam Telelink	Rajasthan	1	

Source: www. trai.gov.in.

It is inferred from Table 3.6 that there are various cellular service providers in the Country.

Circles in Telecom Sectors

The Indian Government classified the Country's Telecom into four circles or Zones based on subscriber potential. These are given below:

Sl. No.	Name of the circle	Areas included
1	Circle 'A'	Maharashtra, Gujarat, Andhra Pradesh, Karnataka and Tamilnadu
2	Circle 'B'	Kerala, Punjab, Haryana, Uttarpradesh, (East & West), Rajasthan, Madhya Pradesh, and Best Bengal
3	Circle 'C'	Himachal Pradesh, Bihar, Orissa, Assam, and North East.
4	Metros 'M'	Delhi, Mumbai, Chennai and Kolkata

Source: Sudhakar and Nutan (2005)[2].

Cellular Telephone Industry in India

The Government of India expressed its interest in inviting private participation to provide cellular services in the Country in 1991. By 1995, licences were awarded for commencement of cellular services in four metro areas of Delhi, Mumbai, Chennai and Kolkata. By 1997-98, cellular services were available in the four Metros and 17 Geographic areas designated as various circles (Jain, 2001). The subscriber-base in 1997 was a mere 3,40,000. In less than ten years, the subscriber-base is poised to touch the 100 million connections mark. The Government's initiative in inviting private participation was aimed at attracting technology and investment from International and Indian players in the Cellular Industry. Thus, "the bidding guidelines mandated foreigner collaboration, and evaluation was based on financial consideration, such as, net worth of partners, licence fee quoted and technical aspects, such as, the subscriber-base experience of the foreign collaborator and network roll-out plan" (Jain, 2001:200). The operators who were successful in the first phase of bidding for cellular licences are listed in Table 3.7. Which also provides the total number of circles each operator won, the all-India market share and subscribers per circle as of the year 2000.

Table 3.7: Status of various Operators 1997-2000

Sl.No.	Operator	No. of Circles	Subscriber Base		Subscribers Per Circle	
			2000	1997	Market Share in%	Subscribers per Circle
1.	Reliance Telecom	7	69,143		37	9.878
2.	BPL Mobile	4	3,41,412	46,240	18.1	85.353
3.	Koshika	4	88,111		4.7	22,028
4.	Aircel Digilink	3	25,476	1,000	1.4	8,492
5.	Escotel	3	1,35,243	2,000	7.2	45,081
6.	JTM	3	94,333	5,598	5.0	31,444
7.	Spice	3	222.908	19,600	11.8	74.303
8.	Bharti	2	188,585	78,723	10.0	94.293
9.	RPG Cellular	2	42,634	12.061	2.3	21.317
10.	Birla AT & T	2	86,397	2,100	4.6	43,199
11.	Aircel	1	40,252		2.1	40,252
12.	Fascel	1	1,09,487	2,000	5.8	1.09,487
13.	Hexacom	1	20,025		1.1	20,025
14.	Hutch	1	1,46,292	63,168	7.8	1,46,292
15.	Skycell	1	25,159	17,335	1.3	25,159
16.	Sterling	1	1,48,220	70,824	7.9	1,48.220
17.	Tat Cellular	1	59,076		3.1	59,076
18.	Usha Martin	1	41,558	18,382	2.2	41,558

Source: Cellular Operators Association in India (COAI), 2000.

Table 3.7 concludes that till the year 2000, all circles including the metros remained duopolies, with the two cellular operators in each circle. In 2000-01, two more players entered each market (or circle). One of these was the State - Owned Bharat Sanchar Nigam Limited (BSNL), which operated the fixed line network in India except the two Metros of Mumbai and Delhi. BSNL, which was a Government Sector Department under the Department of Telecommunications, has been recently corporatized. The second phase of licensing allowed some players to acquire a larger footprint in the Country by way of entry into new markets.

Since the time of inception, the subscriber base (for cellular services with Global System for Mobile GSM) technology) has been growing annually at the compounded rate of 80 per cent. During the early years, the growth was fuelled by increase in subscriber-based in Metro and A Circle markets. In the recent years, the B Circle markets have been catching up fast. By 2006, the subscriber base (for GSM) has grown 200 fold when compared to 1997. The position of various operators in 2006 is given in Table 3.8.

Table 3.8: Status of various Operators 2006

Sl. No.	Operator	No. of Circles	Subscriber Base	Market share in %	Subscriber Per Circle
1.	Bharti	23	1,95,79,208	28.3	8,51,270
2.	BSNL	21	1,71,58,769	24.8	8,17,084
3.	Hutch	9	90,38,271	13.1	10.04,252
4.	Idea	8	73.65,986	10.6	9,20,748
5.	Reliance Telecom	7	18,54, 477	2.7	2,64,925
6.	Dishnet Wireless	5	2,15,156	0.3	43,031
7.	BPL Mobile	4	30,35,285	4.4	7,58,821
8.	Aircel Digilink	3	23,67,591	3.4	7,89,197
9.	Aircel	2	23,96,558	3.5	11,98,279
10.	MTNL	2	19,41,155	2.8	9,70,578
11.	Spcie	2	19,33,408	2.8	9,66,704
12.	Fascel	1	22,57,450	3.3	22,57,450

Table 3.8 explains that the years 2000-01 were critical for the Indian Cellular Industry for yet other reasons, as players consolidated through merges and acquisitions. Many of the Metro Licences and some of the A and B Circle Licences were traded, with many pioneers being acquired by rivals. Consolidation is going on since then. Table 3.11 provides details of various acquisitions and mergers that took place in the Industry. The Industry witnessed many merger / acquisition proposals that were announced, but could not be completed, due to regulatory or other reasons. The top three players, (excluding BSNL) Bharati, Hutch and Idea, were aggressively buying up installed-based and licences. Most of the deals were valued as "price paid per customer" and not in relation to the potential. Thus, the firms that sold their operations to one of their rivals were valued on the basis of the market share they have cornered. In the year 2006, BPL group, which promoted BPL cellular operations exited the business in a deal with the Essar group. It is still not clear who among the existing operators would end up with BPL licences and customers. Table 3.9 deals with the Mergers and Acquisitions in the Indian Cellular Industry.

Table 3.9: Mergers and Acquisitions in the Indian Cellular Industry

Year	Acquired Operator	Buyer	Circles Involved
2001	Sterling	Hutch	Delhi (Metro)
2001	Skycell	Bharti	Chennai(Metro)
2001	Usha Martin	Hutch	Kolkata (Metro)
2001	Spice	Bharti	Kolkata (Metro)
2001	JTM	Bharti	Karnataka(A)
2001	RPG Cellular	Idea	Madhya Pradesh (B)
2003	RPG Cellular	Aircel	Chennai (Metro)
2004	Escotel	Idea	Haryana (B), Uttar Pradesh-West (B), Rajasthan (B), Uttar Pradesh-East, (B), Rajasthan (B), Himachal Pradesh (C)
2005	Hexacom	Bharti	Rajasthan (B), North-East (C)
B: Merger			
Year	**Merged Operators**	**Renamed as**	**Circles involved**
2001	Birla AT & T, Tata Cellular	BATATA-later named idea	Andhra Pradesh, Maharashtra, Gujarat (all A)

Table 3.9 explains that during the years 2001-05, the uncertainty about technology and markets had reduced considerably. Operators started the practice like bundling and price discrimination. Finer market segments were identified and targeted, like youth and college goers, family, long distance callers, small business and so on. The markets were proliferated with many tariff plans to suit the diverse needs of these segments. Value-added services like, web-based applications, e-mail and broadband services were introduced by most operators. The Industry is not just consolidating, but is also maturing in terms of product differentiation and proliferation.

Market Share and Subscriber Base of GSM Service Providers

The important service providers in GSM market are Bharati group, BSNL, Hutch, BPL group, Spice group, Escotel group, Reliance group, MTNL and others. The market share of various service providers and their subscribers base from 2005 to 2007 is given in Table 3.10.

From the Table 3.10, it is inferred that the market share of Bharti group is identified as the highest of GSM service providers with 22.60 per cent in 2007 which is increased from 21.67 per cent in 2005. It is followed by BSNL and Hutch with the market share of 16.38 and 16.36 per cent in 2007 respectively. The market share of Reliance is increased from 19.39 per cent in 2005 to 21.03 per cent in 2007. The total number of subscribers is identified as 33.73 millions in Bharati group during 2007, whereas, in BSNL and Hutch, these were 24.44 and 24.41 millions respectively. The analysis indicates the importance of Bharati group, BSNL, Hutch and Idea group in the GSM market.

Table 3.10: Market Share and Subscriber base of GSM Service Providers

Sl. No.	Cellular group	Number of subscribers in millions			Market share in per cent		
		2005	2006	2007	2005	2006	2007
1.	Bharti group	24.23	28.14	33.73	21.67	21.89	22.60
2.	BSNL	19.06	21.04	24.44	17.05	16.37	16.38
3.	Hutchinson group	18.42	21.16	24.41	16.47	16.46	16.36
4.	Idea group	10.19	11.69	13.07	9.11	9.09	8.76
5.	BPL group	0.82	0.95	1.06	0.73	0.74	0.71
6.	Spice group	1.33	1.57	2.56	1.19	1.22	1.72
7.	Aircel group	3.92	4.16	4.80	3.51	3.24	3.22
8.	Reliance	21.68	26.54	31.39	19.39	20.65	21.03
9.	MTNL	1.83	2.205	2.50	1.64	1.75	1.68
10.	Others	10.33	11.04	11.28	9.24	8.59	7.54
	Total	111.81	128.54	149.24	100.00	100.00	100.00

Source: Cellular Operators' Association of India (COAI), 2008.

Minutes of Usage per Subscriber per Month

It could be seen from Table 3.11 that the average quarterly growth in minutes of usage is positive in all categories of circles for pre-paid and post-paid subscribers, except for post-paid subscribers in the A category of circles. The minutes of usage has registered a negative average growth of -0.31 per cent in the case of A category of circles. The pre-paid and post-paid subscribers in B category and C category of circles have registered a higher growth in comparison with A category and M category of Circles for the studied period. While C category of circles have registered the highest quarterly average growth of 36.44 per cent in minutes of usage in the pre-paid service, the B category circles have registered the highest average quarterly growth in minutes of usage for Pre-paid subscribers is 10.53, 20.58, 36.44 and 10.80 per cent for B, C and M category of circles, respectively. On the other hand, the average quarterly growth of minutes of usage in the case of post-paid subscribers is -0.31, 11.48, 4.47 and 2.39 per cent for A, B, C and M category of circles, respectively.

Table 3.11: Minutes of Usage per Subscriber per month for Pre-paid and post-paid subscribers

Circles category	March 2003	June 2003	September 2003	December 2003	March 2004	Average Quarterly Growth
Pre-paid Subscribers						
A	159	171 (7.55)	217 (26.90)	211 (-2.76)	233 (10.43)	10.53
B	142	142 (0.00)	173 (21.93)	216 (24.86)	293 (35.65)	20.58
C	83	101 (21.69)	127 (25.74)	268 (111.02)	234 (-12.69)	36.44
M	138	179 (29.71)	210 (17.32)	206 (-1.90)	202 (-1.94)	10.80
Post-Paid Subscribers						
A	609	512 (-15.93)	653 (27.54)	589 (-9.80)	571 (-3.06)	-0.31
B	365	529 (44.93)	590 (11.53)	573 (-2.88)	529 (-7.68)	11.48
C	402	378 (-5.97)	398 (5.29)	284 (-28.64)	418 (47.18)	4.47
M	618	632 (2.27)	679 (7.44)	680 (0.15)	678 (-0.29)	2.39

Note: Figures in the parentheses are per cent growth over the previous quarter
Source: Compiled from TRAI (2003-2004).

Proportion of Outgoing Minutes of Usage to in Total Traffic

In order to obtain the outgoing minutes of usage, the proportion of outgoing minutes of usage is computed. In fact, TRAI in its various issues of Indian Telecom Service Performance Indicators provides data on the proportion of the incoming minutes of usage. Using the information on the proportion of incoming minutes in the total traffic, the proportion of outgoing minutes of usage is calculated and presented in Table 3.12.

Table 3.12: Proportion of Outgoing Minutes of usages in total Traffic

Year	March 2003		June 2003		September 2003		December 2003		March 2004	
Circles Category	Pre-paid	Post Paid	Pre-paid	Post Paid	Pre-paid	Post Paid	Pre-paid	Post Paid	Pre-paid	Post Paid
A	NA	NA	29	42	29	44	31	53	27	42
B	NA	NA	27	44	34	47	34	47	31	47
C	NA	NA	27	41	20	47	34	44	34	42
M	NA	NA	24	47	23	45	20	45	19	44
India	27	41	26	45	27	45	28	49	26	44

Note: NA denotes not available.
Source: Computed by using basic data on percentage of incoming minutes of usage, TRAI (2003-2004).

Table 3.12 shows that the proportion of outgoing minutes of usage in the total traffic is greater in all the categories of circles for all the quarters in the case of post-paid subscribers than that of pre-paid subscribers. This shows that the mobile services are mainly used to receive incoming calls in the pre-paid service category. Even in the case of post-paid services, the outgoing minutes of usage is less than 50 per cent in all the cases except for the post-paid subscribers in A category of circle for the quarter ended December 2003, whereas, the proportion of the outgoing minutes in total traffic is 53 per cent.

Outgoing minutes of usage per subscriber per month

It is computed by using the data on the Minutes of Usage (in Table 3.12) and the percentage of outgoing minutes of usage (in Table 3.13). It is defined as the Product of Minutes of Usage Per Subscriber Per Month (MOUPSPM) and Proportion of Outgoing Minutes of Usage (POGMOU) in the total traffic. For the month ended March 2003, the information on the percentage of outgoing call is available only at the national level of aggregation; the outgoing minutes of usage for same period has been arrived at by multiplying the MOUSPSPM with the percentage of outgoing minutes of usage at the national level. Table 3 gives the Outgoing Minutes of Usage (OGMOU) per subscriber per month for pre-paid and post-paid subscribers.

Table 3.13: Outgoing minutes of usage for subscribers

Circles	March 2003	June 2003	September 2003	December 2003	March 2004	Average Quarterly Growth
			Pre-paid Subscribers			
A	42.93	49.905 (16.35)	62.93 (25.99)	65.41 (3.94)	62.91 (-3.82)	10.61
B	38.34	38.34 (0.00)	58.82 (53.42)	73.44 (24.86)	90.83 (23.68)	25.49
C	22.41	27.27 (21.69)	25.4 (-6.86)	91.12 (258.74)	79.56 (-12.69)	65.22
M	252.38	297.04 (17.70)	305.55 (2.86)	306 (0.15)	298.32 (-2.51)	4.55
			Post-paid Subscribers			
A	249.69	215.04 (-13.88)	287.32 (33.61)	312.17 (8.65)	239.82 (-23.18)	1.30
B	149.65	232.76 (55.54)	277.3 (19.14)	269.31 (-2.88)	248.63 (-7.68)	16.12
C	164.82	154.98 (-5.97)	187.06 (20.70)	124.96 (-33.20)	175.56 (40.49)	5.51
M	252.38	297.04 (17.70)	305.55 (2.86)	306 (0.15)	298.32 (-2.51)	4.55

Note: Figures in the parentheses are per cent growth over previous quarter.

Source: Computed from secondary data.

Table 3.13 shows that the outgoing minutes of usage have shown a positive average quarterly growth in all the categories of circles for the pre-paid and post-paid subscribers. The average quarterly growth in the outgoing minutes of usage is higher in B category and C category of circles in comparison with A category and M category of circles. In the case of Pre-paid paid subscribers, the average quarterly growth in the outgoing minutes of usage was 25.49 and 65.22 per cent for B and C category of circles, respectively, whereas, it was 10.61 and 1.55 per cent for A and M category of circles. Similarly, for the post-paid subscribers, the average quarterly growth in the outgoing minutes of usage growth in the outgoing minutes of usage was 16.12 and 5.51 per cent for B category and C category of circles, respectively, whereas, it was 1.30 and 4.55 per cent for A category and M category of circles respectively.

Price Variables for Pre-paid and Post-paid Subscribers

The revenue for the providers of mobile telecom services comes from its different service components, such as, rental revenue, call revenue, roaming revenue, SMS and miscellaneous revenue.

Revenue per subscriber

The data on Revenue Per Subscriber (RPS) are used for arriving at PRPMOU, and CRPMOOGU. The RPS for pre-paid and post-paid subscribers is given in Table 3.14.

Table 3.14: Revenue per subscriber for pre-paid and post-paid mobile services

Circles Category	March 2003	June 2003	September 2003	December 2003	March 2004	Average Quarterly Growth
Revenue Per Subscriber for Pre-paid Services (Rs.)						
A	261	274 (4.98)	334 (21.90)	280 (-14.37)	279 (-2.45)	2.51
B	281	290 (3.20)	309 (6.55)	305 (-1.29)	285 (-6.56)	0.48
C	424	386 (-8.96)	355 (-8.03)	394 (10.99)	346 (-12.18)	-4.55
M	294	293 (-0.34)	297 (1.37)	264 (-11.11)	258 (-2.27)	-3.09
Revenue Per Subscriber for Post-paid Services (Rs.)						
A	1,056	1,051 (-0.47)	1,039 (-1.14)	917 (-11.74)	780 (-14.94)	-7.07
B	796	1,055 (32.54)	1,091 (3.41)	884 (-18.97)	783 (-11.34)	1.39
C	1,973	2,175 (10.24)	1,900 (-12.64)	965 (-49.21)	792 (-17.93)	-17.39
M	1,384	1,340 (-3.18)	1,346 (0.45)	1,348 (0.15)	1,323 (-1.85)	-1.11

Note: Figures in the parentheses are per cent growth over the previous quarter

Source: Compiled from TRAI (2003-2004).

For pre-paid mobile services, the revenue per subscriber has increased in A category and B category of circles at an average quarterly growth rate of 2.51 and 0.48 per cent respectively. However, in the case of C category and M category of circles, it has fallen at the rate of 4.55 and -3.09 per cent, respectively. The average quarterly growth of revenue per subscriber for the post-paid services is 1.39 in B category of circles, whereas, this growth rate is found to be negative for the rest of the categories of circles, such as, A (-7.07), C (-17.39%) and (1.11%).

Revenue Realized per minute of Usage

The ratio of RPS to MOU is equal to the PRPMOU. The Data generated on RRPMOU for the pre-paid and post-paid subscribers are provided in Table 3.15 and 3.16 respectively.

Table 3.15: Revenue realized per minute of usage for Pre-paid Subscribers

Circles Category	March 2003 (Rs.)	June 2003 (Rs.)	September 2003 (Rs.)	December 2003 (Rs.)	March 2004 (Rs.)
A	1.64	1.60 (-2.44)	1.54 (-3.75)	1.36 (-11.69)	1.20 (-11.76)
B	1.98	2.04 (3.03)	1.79 (-12.25)	1.41 (-21.23)	0.97 (-31.21)
C	5.11	3.82 (-25.24)	2.80 (-26.70)	1.47 (-47.50)	1.48 (0.68)
M	2.13	1.64 (-23.00)	1.41 (-14.02)	1.28 (-9.22)	1.28 (0.00)

Note: Figures in the parentheses are per cent growth over previous quarter.
Source: Computed from secondary data.

Table 3.16: Revenue realized per minute of usage for post-paid subscribers

Circles Category	March 2003 (Rs.)	June 2003 (Rs.)	September 2003 (Rs.)	December 2003 (Rs.)	March 2004 (Rs.)
A	1.73	2.05 (18.50)	1.59 (-22.44)	1.56 (-1.89)	1.37 (-12.18)
B	2.18	1.99 (-8.72)	1.85 (-7.04)	1.54 (-16.76)	1.48 (-3.90)
C	4.91	5.75 (17.11)	4.77 (-17.04)	3.40 (-28.72)	1.89 (-44.41)
M	2.24	2.12 (-5.36)	1.98 (-6.60)	1.98 (0.00)	1.95 (-1.52)

Note: Figures in the parentheses are per cent growth over previous quarter.
Source: Computed from secondary data.

The revenue realized per minute of usage for pre-paid subscriber has declined in all the Circles in March 2004 in comparison to March 2003.

However, the pre-paid subscribers of Circle 'C' paid the highest revenue per minute of usage (i.e., ₹ 1.48), while it was lowest in the case of circle 'B' (₹ 0.97) for the quarter ending March 2004.

For the post-paid subscriber, the revenue realized per minute of usage shows a declining trend since September 2003 for all categories of Circles. The quarter ended June 2003 had also registered a fall in the revenue realized per minute of usage over its previous quarter for the circle category 'B' and 'M' The revenue realized per minute of usage was found to be highest for 'M' category of circles, (₹ 1.95) for the quarter ended March 2004, while, the subscribers of 'A' category circles were paying least revenue per minute of usage (₹ 1.37).

Revenue Realized per minute of Outgoing Usage

RRPMOOGU variables have been constructed by using the Call Revenue Per Subscriber Per Month (CRPSPM) and percentage of revenue from call charges at the National Level. The information on percentage of revenue from call charges at the national level is presented in Table 3.17 and 3.18.

Table 3.17: Percentage of revenue from call charges

Year	March 2003		June 2003		September 2003		December 2003		March 2004	
	Pre-paid	Post-paid	Pre-paid	Post-paid	Pre-paid	Post-paid	Pre-paid	Post-paid	Pre-paid	Post-paid
India	57	33	52	29	55	32	68	37	66	40

Source: Compiled from TRAI (2003-2004).

Table 3.18: Call Revenue per subscriber per Month

Circles Category	March 2003 (Rs.)	June 2003 (Rs.)	September 2003 (Rs.)	December 2003 (Rs.)	March 2004 (Rs.)	Average Quarterly Growth
1	2	3	4	5	6	7
			Pre-paid Subscribers			
A	149.71	141.69 (-5.36)	182.97 (29.13)	193.05 (5.51)	184 (-4.69)	6.15
B	161.18	149.96 (-6.96)	169.27 (12.88)	205.88 (21.63)	187.96 (-8.70)	4.71
C	243.21	199.6 (17.93)	194.47 (-2.57)	265.95 (36.76)	228.19 (-14.20)	0.51
M	168.46	151.51 (-10.06)	162.7 (7.39)	178.2 (9.53)	170.15 (-4.52)	0.58
			Post-Paid Subscribers			
A	345.63	306.68 (-11.27)	336.01 (9.56)	338.92 (0.87)	313.09 (-7.62)	-2.12

1	2	3	4	5	6	7
B	260.53	307.85 (18.16)	352.83 (14.61)	326.73 (-7.40)	314.3 (-3.80)	5.39
C	645.76	634.67 (-1.72)	614.46 (.3.18)	356.66 (-41.96)	317.91 (-10.86)	-14.43
M	452.98	391.01 (-13.68)	453.3 (11.33)	498.22 (14.45)	531.05 (6.59)	4.67

Note: Figures in the parentheses are per cent growth over previous quarter.
Source: Computed from secondary data.

The CRPSPM is computed by multiplying the revenue per subscriber per month, with the respective percentage of revenue generated from call charges, the national level of aggregation. It shows that the average quarterly growth in call revenue per subscriber per month is positive for pre-paid subscribers in all the categories of Circles whereas, it is positive only in B category and M category of Circles for the post – paid subscribers. The pre-paid subscribers have an average quarterly growth rate of 6.15, 4.71, 0.51 and 0.58 per cent for A, B, C and M category of Circles, respectively. In the case of post-paid subscribers B and M category of Circles shows the quarterly growth rate of 5.39 and 4.67 respectively.

Marketing Strategy Framework of Cellular Operator

Airtel (Market Leader)

With a 27.2 per cent market share, Airtel has emerged as a Market Leader. Bharti Televentures have positioned themselves as integrated players, with a desire to have a presence in basic (both wire line and wireless) as well as National and International Long Distance.

Hutch/BSNL (market challengers)

Hutch, with a 18.9 per cent market share, has followed a differentiation, strategy by offering its Customers Value Added Service (VAS). They have followed a top-down approach, tapping category A cities. BSNL is a state-owned player with a market share of 22.6 per cent and has been able to leverage its low cost position in small towns and Sec. B and Sec. C Cities.

Idea (market follower)

With a 12.4 per cent market share, it has positioned itself as a 'value for money' brand. It simply follows the leader and the challenger after the technology becomes successful.

Spice/Shyam Telecom/Reliance/Aircel (Market Nichers)

They are the nichers who cater to very small niche markets, not served by the big players.

REFERENCES

1. www. Supercommindia 2004. com/Indian_t_sehtm (2002 figures).
2. Francis Sudhakar, K. and Lydia Nutan, (2005), "An objective study of customer behaviour in BPL Mobile Cellular Ltd", *Indian Journal of Marketing, 35(5),* May, p.10.

Customer's Profile and their Preference on the Service Provider in GSM Market

Introduction

In this Chapter, the researcher has analysed the customer's perception on the services offered by the various service providers, since it is virtually important for analyzing the impact of marketing strategies adopted by the various service providers. The service quality is more important in the Indian Mobile Phone Service Sector. The service quality analysis has been discussed by some Researchers (Prahad and Ramasamy, 2004)[1]. They identified the importance of service quality and also the service quality gap to be filled up by appropriate marketing strategy. The customers' satisfaction is the ultimate aim of any marketers (Yi, 1990)[2]. The satisfaction may be related to product attitude, sales personnel and a consumption experience (Oliver, 1981)[3].

Customer's Perception on the Services Quality of the Services Providers

The extreme level of customer satisfaction leads to customers' delight and loyalty. Every service provider in any industry expects this customer loyalty.

In order to create the customer loyalty, it is highly essential to analyse the customer's behaviour with regular intervals, since there is a frequent change in the customer's behaviour and the environment. Then only they can formulate appropriate marketing strategy. Hence the present study has made an attempt on analyzing the customer's attitudes towards the variables influencing the choice of the service provider, switching intention, service quality of service providers, overall satisfaction and customers loyalty in the market. Initially, in order to provide the background of customers, their profiles have been revealed.

Age Among the Customers

The age among the customers plays an important role in the expectation and perception on various services offered by the mobile phone service providers. Usually, the youngsters are having more knowledge on the various attributes and facilities related to the mobile phone services than the elders. Hence, age is included as one of the profile variables in the present study. The age among the customers is confined to less than 25 years, 25 to 35 years, 36 to 45 years; 46 to 55 years and above 55 years. The distribution of customers on the basis of their age is given in Table 4.1.

Table 4.1: Age among the Customers

Sl. No.	Age (in years)	Number of Customers in	Per cent to the Total
1.	Less than 25	161	23.23
2.	25-35	252	36.36
3.	36-45	168	24.24
4.	46-55	69	9.96
5.	Above 55	43	6.21
	Total	693	100.00

Source: Primary data.

Table 4.1 explains that the important age group among the customers are 25 to 35 and 36 to 45 years, which contribute 36.36 and 24.24 per cent to the total. The customer's age of less than 25 years constitutes 23.23 per cent to the total. The customers are grouped into youngsters and elders. The youngsters who are in the age of 35 and less than 35 years old, whereas, the elders are those who are in the age of 36 and above 36 years old. The youngsters in the present study constitute 59.59 per cent to the total. The elders constitute 40.41 per cent to the total.

Distribution of Customers on the Basis of the Service Providers

The important service providers in Kanniyakumari District are Airtel, Aircel, BSNL, (Hutch) Vodafone, Idea and others. It is imperative to analyse the distribution of customers on the basis of their service providers in order to analyse their loyalty, switching behaviour, expectation and perception on the service quality of the service providers. The distribution on that sampled customers on the basis of their service providers is presented in Table 4.2.

Table 4.2 explains that the important service providers among the customers in the study are BSNL and Airtel which constitute 25.39 and 23.81 per cent total. The customers of Airtel constitute 20.78 per cent to the total. The service providers are classified into two important categories, namely, youngsters and elders. The important service provider among the youngsters is Airtel and Aircel which constitutes 23.24 and 22.02 per cent to its total. The most important service providers among the elders are BSNL and Airtel, which constitutes 32.14 and 24.64 per cent to its total respectively. The new customers, namely, Idea and spice are very popular among the youngsters than the elders.

Table 4.2: Distribution of Customers on the Basis of Services Providers

Sl. No.	Name of the Service Providers	Number of Customers in		Total
		Youngsters	Elders	
1.	Airtel	96	69	165
2.	Aircel	91	53	144
3.	BSNL	86	90	176
4.	Vodafone	69	32	101
5.	Idea	44	19	63
6.	Others	27	17	44
	Total	**413**	**280**	**693**

Source: Primary data

Gender among the Customers

Gender is one of the important profiles of the customers. Since the sex of the customers may have its own influence on the perception on various attributes related mobile phone service, it is included as one of the important profile variables. The distinction of customers as the basis of their sex is given in Table 4.3.

Table 4.3: Gender among the customers

Sl. No.	Gender	Number of Customers in		Total
		Youngsters	Elders	
1.	Male	309	178	487
2.	Female	104	102	206
	Total	**413**	**280**	**693**

Source: Primary data

The male customer constitutes 70.27 per cent to the total. The important gender among the youngsters and elders are male, which constitutes 74.82 and 63.57 per cent to its total respectively. The analysis infers that the important gender among the customers in the study is 'male'.

Level of Education among the Customers

Since the level of education indicates the level of knowledge, understanding and analytical capability of the customers, it is included as one of the profile variables. The highly educated customers may have more knowledge and ideas on the mobile phone service market. Hence, their level of expectation and perception are completely different from others. In the present study, the level of education among the customers is classified into school level, higher secondary level, under graduation, post graduation, professional and others. The distribution of customers on the basis of their level of education is shown in Table 4.4.

Table 4.4: Level of education among the Customers

Sl.No.	Level of Education	Number of Customers in		Total
		Youngsters	Elders	
1.	School Level	42	29	71
2.	Higher Secondary	83	27	110
3.	Under Graduation	129	106	235
4.	Post Graduation	71	46	117
5.	Professional	66	37	103
6.	Others	22	35	67
	Total	**413**	**280**	**693**

Source: Primary data

Table 4.4 explains that in total, a maximum of 33.91 per cent of the customers are having a level of education of under graduation, which is followed by 16.88 per cent of the customers, which the level of education of post graduation level. The number of customers with professional education constitutes 14.86 per cent to the total. The first two important level of education among the youngsters are under-graduation and higher secondary which constitutes 31.23 and 20.09 per cent to its total, respectively. Among the elders, these two are under-graduation and post graduation which constitute 37.86 and 16.43 per cent to its total. The analysis reveals that the level of education among the youngsters and elders are better in the study area. The professional education is identified as higher among the youngsters than the elders.

Marital Status among the Customers

Since the marital status has its own influences on the perceptions on the various aspects in mobile phone services, it is included as one of the profile variables. The marital status among the customers in the present study is

Table 4.5: Marital status among the Customers

Sl.No.	Marital Status	Number of Customers in		Total
		Youngsters	Elders	
1.	Unmarried	182	7	189
2.	Recently Married	163	18	181
3.	Married	68	235	303
4.	Separated	–	12	12
5.	Widow/Widower	–	8	8
	Total	**413**	**280**	**693**

Source: Primary data

confined to the unmarried, the recently married, the married, the separated and the widows/widowers. The distribution of the customers on the basis of their marital status is illustrated in Table 4.5.

Table 4.5 shows that in total, a maximum of 43.72 per cent of the customers are married, which is followed by unmarried customers, who contributed 27.27 per cent to the total. The recently married customers constitute 26.12 per cent to the total. The first two groups of marital status among the youngsters are unmarried and recently married which constitute 44.06 and 39.47 per cent to the total, respectively. Among the elders, these two are married and recent married which constitutes, 83.93 and 6.43 per cent to the total respectively. The analysis infers that the important marital status among the respondents is married, unmarried, and recently married.

Occupation among the Customers

The occupation represents the nature of work or occupation engaged by the customers. Since the nature of occupation may have its own influence on the selection of service providers and also the perception and expectation on various services offered by the service providers, it is included as one of the profile variables. The present study classifies the occupational background of the customers into students, housewives, Government employees, private employees, businessman and others. The occupational background among the customers is shown in Table 4.6.

Table 4.6: Occupation among the Customers

Sl. No.	Occupation	Number of Customers in		Total
		Youngsters	Elders	
1.	Students	151	–	151
2.	Housewife	32	21	53
3.	Government Employment	48	64	112
4.	Private Employment	71	82	153
5.	Business	76	71	147
6.	Others	35	42	77
	Total	**413**	**280**	**693**

Source: Primary data

Table 4.6 portrays that the important occupation among the customer is private employment, students and business, which constitute 22.07, 21.79, 23.78 and 21.21 per cent to the total. The number of housewives constitutes 7.64 per cent to the total, whereas, the number of Government employees constitutes 16.16 per cent, to the total. The important occupation among the youngsters is students and business which constitutes 36.56 and 18.40 per cent to its total respectively. Among the elders, these two are private employment and business which constitute 29.29 and 25.36 per cent to its total, respectively. The analysis reveals that important occupation among the respondent are private employment, students and business.

Family Size among The Customers

The family size among the customers indicates the number of family members living along with the customers. Since the family size among the customers may have its own role in the selection of the service providers, it is included as one of the profile of the customers. The family size among the customers is confined to less than 3; 3 to 4; 5 to 6; 7 to 8 and above 8. The distribution of customers according their family size is shown in Table 4.7.

Table 4.7: Family size among the Customers

Sl. No.	Family size	Number of Customers in		Total
		Youngsters	Elders	
1.	Less than 3	65	34	99
2.	3-4	137	124	261
3.	5-6	140	62	202
4.	7-8	42	48	90
5.	Above 8	29	12	41
	Total	**413**	**280**	**693**

Source: Primary data.

From Table 4.7 it is concluded that the important family size among the customers are 3 to 4 and 5 to 6 members, which constitute 37.66 and 29.15 per cent to the total. The number of customers with the family size of less than 3 members constitute 14.29 per cent to the total. The important types of family size among the youngsters are 5 to 6 and 3 to 4 members which constitute 33.89 and 33.17 per cent to its total respectively. Among the elder customers these two are 3 to 4 and 5 to 6 members, which constitute 44.28 and 22.14 per cent, to its total respectively. The analysis infers that the family size among the customers are ranging from 3 to 6 members per family.

Personal Income among The Customers

It indicates the income derived by the customers through all possible sources of income available to them. Since the personal income among the customers may influence more the selection of mobile phone service provider and also in analyzing their service quality, it is included as one of the profile variables. The personal income among the customers in the present study is classified into less than ‘4,000; ‘4,000 to ‘8,000; ‘8,001 to 12,000; ‘12001 to 16,000 and above ‘16,000. The distribution of customers on the basis of their personal income is explained in Table 4.8.

Table 4.8: Personal income per month Among the Customers

Sl. No.	Personal Incme	Number of Customers in		Total
		Youngsters	Elders	
1.	Less than '4,000	63	24	87
2.	4,000-8,000	78	27	105
3.	8,000-12,000	110	50	160
4.	12,000-16,000	96	84	180
5.	Above 16,000	66	95	161
	Total	**413**	**280**	**693**

Source: Primary data

The important personal incomes among the customers, in the present study are '12,000 to 16,000, and above '16,000 which constitute 25.97 and 23.23 per cent to the total, respectively. The number of customers with the personal income of less than '4,000 constitutes 12.55 per cent to the Total. The first two important personal incomes among the youngsters are '8,001 to 12,000 and '12001 to 16,000 which constitute 26.63 and 23.24 per cent to the total respectively. Among the elders, the first two personal incomes are above '16,000 and '12,000 to 16,000, which constitute 33.93 and 30.00 per cent to the total respectively. The analysis reveals that the average personal incomes among the elder are greater than the youngsters.

Number of Earning Members Per Family

It represents the total number of earning members per family of the customers. Since it has its own influence on their perception and expectation on the services provided by the various service providers, it is included as one of the profile variables in the present study. The number of earning members per family is confined to one, two, three and four above three in the present study. The distribution of customers on the basis of the number of earning members per family is given in Table 4.9.

Table 4.9: Number of earning members per family among the Customers

Sl. No.	Number of earning members per family	Number of Customers in		Total
		Youngsters	Elders	
1.	One	148	105	253
2.	Two	186	93	279
3.	Three	49	60	109
4.	More than Three	30	22	52
	Total	**413**	**280**	**693**

Source: Primary data.

The important number of earning members per family among the customers is two and one, which constitutes 40.26 and 36.51 per cent to the total, respectively. The customers with the earning members of more than three per family constitute 7.50 per cent to the total. The important number of earning members per family among the young customers is two and one, which constitutes 45.03 and 35.84 per cent to its total, respectively. Among the elder customers, these two are one and two which constitute 37.50 and 33.21 per cent to its total, respectively.

Family Income among the Customers

The family income among the customers represents the total income earned by all earning members in the household. Since the family income is one of the important factors that determines the standard of living of the people, it is included as one of the profile variables. The better standard of living of the people many influence their level of thinking and knowledge on the various attributes of the mobile phone service. The family income per month among the customers is confined to less than '6,000; '6000 to 12,000; '12001 to '18,000; '18,001 to 24,000 and above 24,000. The distribution of customers on the basis of their family income is presented in Table 4.10.

Table 4.10: Family income among the Customers

Sl. No.	Personal Income	Number of Customers in		Total
		Youngsters	Elders	
1.	Less than 6,000	52	11	63
2.	6,000-12,000	52	39	91
3.	12,001-18,000	126	65	191
4.	18,001-24,000	119	86	205
5.	Above 24,000	64	79	143
	Total	**413**	**280**	**693**

Source: Primary data

From Table 4.10, it is inferred that in total, a maximum of 29.58 per cent of the customers are having a family income of '18,001 to 24,000, which is followed by 27.56 per cent of the customers with the family income of '12,001 to 18,000. The number of customers with the family income of above '12,001 to 18,000. The number of customers with the family income of above 24,000 constitutes 20.63 per cent to the total. The important family income among the youngsters are '12,001 to 18,000 and '18,001 to 24,000 which constitutes 30.51 and 28.87 per cent to its total, respectively. Among the elders, these two family incomes are '18,001 to 24,000 and above '24,000 which constitute 30.71 and 28.21 per cent to its total, respectively. The analysis infers that the family income per month among the elders are greater than among elders.

Personality of the Customers

The personality trait of the customers represents the way of behaviour, interaction, understanding and other psychological aspects of the customers. The personality of the customers has been measured through so many variables in practice. In the present study, these are measured with the help of sociability, media exposure, innovativeness, scientific orientation, and risk orientation among the customers. The relevant statements in each aspect have been identified with the help of previous reviews and views of experts.

Sociability among the Customers

It represents the social interaction of the customers. It reveals how the customers interact with the society. In the practical life, the customers have to interact with so many persons in the society. The level of interaction with the society may provide more knowledge and analytical capability of the services offered by the service provider. In the present Study, the level of sociability among the customers is measured with the help of some related statements. The customers are asked to rate these statements at five point scale. The level of sociability is computed by the mean score of the variables in the sociability. It is confined to less than 2.0; 2.00 to 3.00; 3.01 to 4.00 and above 4.00. The distribution of customers on the basis of their level of sociability is given in Table 4.11.

Table 4.11: Level of Sociability among the Customers

Sl. No.	Level of sociability	Number of Customers in		Total
		Youngsters	Elders	
1.	Less than 2.0	22	71	93
2.	2.0-3.00	82	69	151
3.	3.0-4.00	143	83	226
4.	Above 4.00	166	57	223
	Total	**413**	**280**	**693**

Source: Primary data.

The important level of sociability among the customers is 3.0 to 4.00 and above 4.00 which constitutes 32.61 and 32.18 per cent to the total, respectively. The customers with the score of sociability of less than 2.0 constitutes 13.42 per cent to the total. The important level of sociability among the youngsters is above 4.00 and 3.00 to 4.00 which constitutes 40.19 and 34.62 per cent to its total, respectively. Among the elder customers, these are 3.00 to 4.00 and less than which constitutes 29.64 and 25.35 per cent to its total respectively. The analysis reveals that the level of sociability among the youngsters are greater than among the elder customers.

Level of media exposure among the Customers

It represents the level of exposure with the different media of the customers. The higher level of media exposure may increase their level of expectation and perception on the service quality of services offered by the providers. In the present Study, the level of media exposure among the customers has been measured with the help of relevant statements. The level of media exposure among the customers is confined to less than 2.0; 2.00 to 3.00; 3.01 to 4.00 and above 4.00. The distribution of customers on the basis of their level of media exposure is given in Table 4.12.

Table 4.12: Level of media exposure among the Customers

Sl. No.	Level of Media Exposure	Number of Customers in		Total
		Youngsters	Elders	
1.	Less than 2.0	23	52	75
2.	2.0-3.0	44	72	116
3.	3.01 to 4.0	119	85	204
4.	Above 4.00	227	71	298
	Total	**413**	**280**	**693**

Source: Primary data.

The important level of media exposure among the customers is above 4.00 and 3.01 to 4.00, which constitute 43.00 and 29.44 per cent to the total, respectively. The important level of media exposure among the young customers are above 4.00 and 3.01 to 4.00, which constitutes 54.96 and 28.81 per cent to its total, respectively. Among the elder customers, these are 3.01 to 4.00 and 2.0 to 3.00, which constitute 30.36 and 25.71 per cent to its total, respectively. The level of media exposure is identified as higher among the young customers compared to elder customers.

Level of Innovativeness among the Customers

It represents the level of acceptance of new things and changes in the economy among the customers. The higher level of innovativeness may lead to better awareness and knowledge on any aspects among the customers. The level of innovativeness among the customers has been measured with the help of some related statements, which are measured at five point scale. The level of innovativeness among the customers is confined to less than 2.0; 2.00 to 3.00; 3.01 to 4.00 and above 4.00. The distribution of customers on the basis of their level of innovativeness is illustrated in Table 4.13.

The important level of innovativeness among the customers is 3.01 to 4.00 and above 4.00 which constitutes 37.60 and 32.32 per cent to the total, respectively. The important levels of innovativeness among the young customer are 3.01 to 4.0 and above 4.0 which constitute 44.31 and 33.66

per cent to their total, respectively. Among the elder customers, these levels are above 4.00 and 3.01 to 4.00, which constitute 30.36 and 27.86 per cent to their total, respectively.

Table 4.13: Level of Innovativeness among the Customers

Sl. No.	Level of innovativeness	Number of Customers in		Total
		Youngsters	Elders	
1.	Less than 2.0	20	48	68
2.	2.0-3.0	71	69	140
3.	3.01-4.0	183	78	261
4.	Above 4.00	139	85	224
	Total	**413**	**280**	**693**

Source: Primary data.

Scientific orientation among the Customers

The scientific orientation among the customers indicates the level of application of scientific principles in their consumption among the customers. It reveals the ways and means of achieving maximum satisfaction with minimum price. The level of scientific orientation among the customers is measured by some relevant statements, which are measured by at five point scale. The level of scientific orientations is confined to less than 2.0; 2.00 to 3.00; 3.01 to 4.00 and above 4.00. The distribution of customers on the basis of their level of scientific orientation is illustrated in Table 4.14.

Table 4.14: Level of scientific orientation among the Customers

Sl. No.	Level of scientific orientation	Number of Customers in		Total
		Youngsters	Elders	
1.	Less than 2.0	114	72	186
2.	2.0-3.00	168	132	300
3.	3.01-4.00	86	42	128
4.	Above 4.00	45	34	79
	Total	**413**	**280**	**693**

Source: Primary data

The important levels of scientific orientation among the customers are 2.00 to 3.00 and less than 2.00, which constitute 43.29 and 26.84 per cent to their total, respectively. The customers with the score of above 4.00 constitute 11.40 percent to the total. The important level of scientific orientation among the young customers is 2.00 to 3.00 and less than 2.00, which constitutes 40.68 and 27.60 per cent to its total, respectively. Among the elder customers, these are 2.00 to 3.00 and less than 2.00 which constitute 47.14 and 25.71 per cent to their total, respectively.

Risk orientation among the Customers

The level of risk orientation among the customers indicates their capability and willingness to take risk in their consumption or other activities. The level of risk orientation among the customers has been measured with the help of some relevant statements, which are measured at five point scale. The Levels of risk orientation among the customers are confined to less than 2.0; 2.0 to 3.0; 3.01 to 4.00 and above 4.0. The distribution of customers on the basis of their level of risk orientation is given in Table 4.15.

Table 4.15: Level of risk orientation among the Customers

Sl. No.	Level of risk orientation	Number of Customers in		Total
		Youngsters	Elders	
1.	Less than 2.0	72	102	174
2.	2.0-3.0	102	73	175
3.	3.01-4.00	143	45	188
4.	Above 4.00	96	60	156
	Total	**413**	**280**	**693**

Source: Primary data.

The important level of risk orientation among the customers is 3.01 to 4.00 and 2.00 to 3.00, which constitutes 27.13 and 25.25 per cent to the total, respectively. The important level of risk orientation among the young customers is 3.01 to 4.00 and 2.00 to 3.00, which constitutes 34.62 and 24.69 per cent to its total, respectively. Among the elder customers, these are less than 2.00 and 2.00 3.00, which constitute 36.43 and 26.07 per cent to their total, respectively. The analysis reveals that the level of risk orientation among the young customers is greater than among the elder customers.

Personality score (PSO) among the Customers

The personality score (PSO) of the customers has been computed by the mean score of the variables related to the personality traits of the customers. The PSO of the customers in the present study is confined to less than 2.0; 2.00 to 3.00; 3.01 to 4.00 and above 4.00. The distribution of customers on the basis of PSO is illustrated in Table 4.16.

The important PSO among the customers is 2.0 to 3.00 and 3.00 to 4.00 which constitutes 32.61 and 28.14 per cent to the total, respectively. The customers with the PSO of above 4.00 constitute 17.75 per cent to the total. The important PSO among the young customers is 2.0 to 3.00 and 3.01 to 4.00, which constitutes 33.66 and 30.51 per cent to its total, respectively. Among the elder customers, these are less than 2.0 and 2.0 to 3.0 which constitute 36.43 and 31.07 per cent to their total. The analysis reveals that the personality of the young customers is greater than the elder customers.

Table 4.16: Personality score (PSO) among the Customers

Sl. No.	PSO	Number of Customers in		Total
		Youngsters	Elders	
1.	Less than 2.0	47	102	149
2.	2.0-3.0	139	87	226
3.	3.01 – 4.0	126	69	195
4.	Above 4.00	101	22	123
	Total	**413**	**280**	**693**

Source: Primary data.

Number of Mobile Phones used at the Household

It represents the number of mobile phone handsets used by the family members in the household. Since the number of handsets used by the household leads to more knowledge on the various services offered by the service providers in mobile phone industry, it is also included as one of the profile variables. In the present study, the number of mobile phones used in the household is classified into one, two, three, four and above four. The distribution of customers on the basis of the number of mobile phone used in their household is given in Table 4.17.

Table 4.17: Number of mobile phones used at the Household

Sl. No.	Number of Mobile Phones	Number of Customers in		Total
		Youngsters	Elders	
1.	One	150	104	254
2.	Two	169	91	260
3.	Three	48	43	91
4.	Four	34	42	76
5.	Above Four	12	-	12
	Total	**413**	**280**	**693**

Source: Primary data

Table 4.17 concludes that in total, a maximum of 37. 52 per cent of the customers households are using two mobile phones per household. It is followed by 36.65 per cent of the households using one mobile phone per household. In the case of youngsters, the first two number of mobile phones used per household are two and one which constitute 40.92 and 36.32 per cent to their total, respectively. In the case of elders, these two are one and two, which constitute 37.14 and 32.50 per cent to their total respectively.

Brand Preference Regarding Handsets by The Customers

The handset preferred by the customers may be optional or compulsory. In the case of GSM market, the customers are having full freedom to choose the handset, as they like. Eventhough, the existing brands of handsets are too many, the present study limits itself to Nokia, L.G, Samsung, Sony, Motorola, Reliance, Tata and others. The brand of handset preferred by the customers is given in Table 4.18.

Table 4.18: Brand of handset among the Customers

Sl. No.	Family size	Number of Customers in		Total
		Youngsters	Elders	
1.	Nokia	163	142	305
2.	LG	21	18	39
3.	Samsung	48	21	69
4.	Sony	42	19	61
5.	Motorola	51	26	77
6.	Reliance	22	17	39
7.	Tata	16	8	24
8.	Others	50	29	79
	Total	**413**	**280**	**693**

Source: Primary data.

Table 4.18 reveals that the dominant brand of handset preferred by the customers is Nokia, which constitutes 44.01 per cent to the total. It is followed by others (China sets) and Motorola which constitute 11.39 and 11.11 per cent to the total, respectively. The important brand of handsets preferred by the youngsters is Nokia and Motorola, which constitute 39.47 and 12.35 per cent to its total, respectively. Among the elders, these are Nokia and others, which constitute 50.71 and 10.36 per cent to their total respectively. The analysis reveals the dominance of Nokia handset among the customers.

Purpose of using the Mobile Phone Services

It infers the purpose of using the mobile phone services among the customers in the market. Eventhough, the purpose of using the services are too many, the present Study narrows it down to twelve purposes. The customers are asked to the given purposes at five point scale from highly important to not at all important. The assigned marks on these scales are from 5 to 1 respectively. In order to exhibit the important purpose of using mobile phone services, the mean score of each purpose among the youngster and elder customers has been computed separately. In order to find out the significant difference among the two groups of customers regarding the attitude on the purposes, the 't' test has been administered.

Table 4.19 explains the mean score of purposes and its respective 't' statistics. The important purposes mentioned by the young customers in the market are symbol of status, convenience and multi purpose, since their

Table 4.19: Purpose of using Cell phone Service

Sl. No.	Purpose	Number of Customers in		Total
		Youngsters	Elders	
1.	Security	3.7813	3.4232	0.5147
2.	SMS	3.2608	3.5033	-0.4108
3.	Official	2.6873	3.8142	-3.1173*
4.	Touch with friends and Relatives	3.3089	3.1141	0.4099
5.	Symbol of Status	3.9183	3.0672	2.5762*
6.	Convenience	3.8844	3.2166	1.8084
7.	Low Cost	2.5783	3.5162	-3.9188*
8.	Passion	2.7086	3.0096	-0.6862
9.	STD Calls	2.8544	3.6864	-2.0981*
10.	Dissatisfaction with land line	3.1443	2.3068	1.9897*
11.	Multipurpose	3.8667	2.8081	2.1786*
12.	Easy to contact	2.9193	3.2667	-0.6807

Source: Primary data
*Significant at five per cent level.

respective mean scores are 3.9183, 3.8844 and 3.8667. Among the elder customers in the market, these purposes are official, STD calls and low cost, since their respective mean scores are 3.8142, 3.6864 and 3.5162. Regarding the perception on various purposes, the significant difference among the two groups of customers has been identified in the perception on official, status symbol, low cost, STD calls, dissatisfaction with the landline and multipurpose since the 't' statistics are significant at five per cent level.

Source of Information about the Service Provider

The customers may have different sources of information about their service providers. The source of information about the service providers is more important for some policy implications related to the media of communication and advertisement about the service providers. It is also useful to identify the powerful source of communication among the youngsters and elders. It is included in the present Study, Eventhough, the services of information are too many, the present Study confines these sources to salesman, advertisement, promotional measure, friends and relatives; posters and displays; company retailers and distributors. The customers are asked to rate the source of information at five point scale from highly important, to not at all important. The assigned marks on these scales are from 5 to 1 respectively. The mean score of source of information among the young and elder customers in GSM market has been computed separately.

Table 4.20: Source of information about the Service Providers

Sl. No.	Source of Information	Mean Score among Customers in		Total
		Youngsters	Elders	
1.	Salesmen	3.8568	2.7108	2.4568*
2.	Advertisement	3.0869	3.9117	-2.1173*
3.	Promotional Measure	3.7163	3.4562	0.4566
4.	Friends and Relatives	2.9198	3.3068	-0.7108
5.	Posters and Displays	3.1414	3.2962	-0.3906
6.	Company	2.6862	3.8238	-2.6091
7.	Retailers	3.8081	3.0617	-2.6091
8.	Distributors	3.9195	3.1472	2.0856*

Source: Primary data.
*Significant at five per cent level.

Table 4.20 explains the mean score of different sources of information among the customers in GSM market. The significant difference among the two groups of customers has been examined with the help of 't' test. The highly perceived source of information among the young customers is Distributors, Salesmen, and Retailers, since the respective mean scores are 3.9185, 3.8568 and 3.8081. Among the elder customers in GSM market, these sources of information are advertisement, company and promotional measures, since the respective mean scores are 3.9117, 3.8238 and 3.4562. Regarding the perception on the sources of information about the service providers, the significant difference among the two group of customers has been identified in the perception on Salesmen, Advertisement, Company Retailers and Distributors, since the respective 't' statistics are significant at five per cent level.

Variables Influencing the Choice of the Service Providers

The service provider in the mobile phone service market is chosen with the assessment of various variables related to the attributes of the services offered by the provider. The customers in the mobile phone market are generally knowledgeable and the youth. Hence, they are better informed on the mobile phone services and also the service providers. Only after the evaluation of various variables related to the service providers, they choose a particular service provider or they switch from one service provider to another. Even though the variables leading to the choice of the service in mobile phone market are too many, the present Study narrows down these variables to free incoming facility, nominal charges on calls, network coverage, free SMS facility, frequent schemes, voice clarity, prepaid/post paid facility, low cost SIM cards, brand image, call waiting facility, large number of promotional schemes, inter-network coverage, low activation charges, multi-media messaging facility, goodwill of the provider, natural roaming facility, minimum security amount, lesser office formalities, positive words of mouth, increased validity period, higher number of included minutes, special/festival offer, reasonable charges on outgoing calls, classification of peak and off peak hours, good in house coverage, multi-national company and itemized billing. The customers are asked to rate the abovesaid twenty seven variables at five point scale from highly disagree according to the importance given to that variable to choose the service provider. The assigned marks on these scales are from 5 to 1 respectively. The mean score of the variables among the young and older customers in GSM market has been computed separately to show the importance of the variables. The significant difference among the two group of customers has been analysed with the help of 't' test. The results are given in Table 4.21.

Table 4.21: Variables influencing the choice of the Present Service Provider

Sl. No.	Variables	Mean Score among Customers in		Total
		Youngsters	Elders	
1	2	3	4	5
1.	Free incoming facility	3.1817	3.9297	-2.3089*
2.	Nominal charges on calls	3.6086	2.5631	2.7182*
3.	Network coverage	3.9198	3.1091	2.0818*
4.	Free SMS facility	3.0644	3.9193	2.1306*
5.	Frequent Schemes	2.4563	3.0841	-1.3114
6.	Voice Clarity	3.8681	3.6139	1.4049
7.	Prepaid/Postpaid facility	3.7029	3.0321	2.1142*
8.	Low cost SIM card	3.9193	2.4562	3.1108*
9.	Brand Image	3.0611	3.8684	2.1973*
10.	Call waiting facility	3.8162	3.2311	-0.6899
11.	Large number of promotional schemes	3.5086	3.6032	-0.1147
12.	Inter-Network coverage	3.9193	3.6994	-2.8033*
13.	Low activation charges	2.9017	3.8641	-2.3917*
14.	Multi-media messaging facility	3.6904	2.8962	1.9686*
15.	Goodwill of the provider	3.5611	3.8164	-0.7108
16.	Natural Roaming facility	3.7088	3.9144	-0.3149
17.	Minimum security amount	3.2611	3.6783	-0.8084
18.	Lesser office formalities	2.9197	3.6441	-1.9203

1	2	3	4	5
19.	Positive words of mouth	3.3044	32.2661	2.4146*
20.	Increased validity period	2.9197	3.6441	-1.9203
21.	Higher Number of included minutes	3.2444	3.3086	-0.3117
22.	Special/festival offer	3.6897	2.8681	1.9703*
23.	Reasonable charges on outgoing calls	3.7081	3.8082	-0.1317
24.	Classification of peak and off peak hours	2.9694	3.1763	-0.2614
25.	Good in house coverage	3.1144	3.8143	-1.5068
26.	Multi-national company	2.7178	2.8681	-0.2368
27.	Itemized Billing	3.4563	2.6444	0.8685

Source: Primary data

*Significant at five per cent level.

From Table 4.21, it is concluded that the highly perceived variables among the young customers in GSM market are network coverage, low cost SIM card and voice clarity, since the respective mean scores are 3.9198, 3.9193 and 3.8681. Among the elder customers in GSM market, these variables are inter network coverage, free incoming facility and national roaming facility, since the respective mean scores are 3.9694, 3.9297 and 3.9144. Regarding the perception on the variables leading to the selection of the service providers, the significant difference among the two group of customers has been identified in the perception on free incoming facility, nominal charges on calls, network coverage, free SMS facility, prepaid/ postpaid facility, low cost SIM card, brand image, inter network coverage, low activation charges, multi-media messaging facility, positive word of mouth and special/festival offer, since the respective 't' statistics are significant at five per cent level.

Factors Influencing the Choice of the Service Providers

The variables influencing the choice of the service provider are narrated with the help of Exploratory Factor Analysis (EFA) for further indepth analysis. Before applying the factor analysis, the data validity of factor analysis is tested with the help of Kaiser-meyer-ohlin (KMO) measure of sampling adequacy and Bartletts test of sphericity. The minimum acceptable KMO measure is 0.5, whereas, the level of significance in Chi-square test is at 5 per cent level. The above two conditions are satisfied by the KMO measure of the present Study (0.7108) and the Zero per cent level of significance of chi-square test. The score of the variables leading to the service provider has been included for the EFA. The factor analysis results in five important factors leading to select the present service provider. The number of variables included in each factor, its reliability coefficient, eigen value and the per cent of variation explained by each factor are summarized in Table 4.22.

Table 4.22: Factors influencing to select the Service Provider

Sl. No.	Factors	Variables	Eigen Value	Per cent of Variation explained	Cronbach alpha
1.	Service	8	4.1103	26.18	0.8484
2.	Economy	6	2.9068	16.73	0.7836
3.	Coverage	5	2.6665	12.79	0.8081
4.	Scheme	4	2.0114	10.68	0.7668
5.	Image	4	1.8661	8.17	0.7968
	Total	**27**		**74.55**	
	KMO measure of sampling Adequacy: 0.8219			Bartletts test of sphericity: Chi-square value: 97.07*	

*Significant at five per cent level.

From Table 4.22, it is revealed that the narrated five factors explain the variables leading to the choice of the service provider to the extent of 74.55 per cent. The important factor identified by the factor analysis is 'service', since its eigen value is 4.1103. It is followed by the factors, namely, economy and coverage with the eigen value of 2.9068 and 2.6665, respectively. The last two factors narrated by the factor analysis are scheme and image since the eigen value are 2.0114 and 1.8681, respectively.

Standardized Factor loading of the Variables in 'service' Factor

In total, there are eight variables in the service factor, since the factor loadings with the service factor are higher than the factor loadings with other factors. The score of the eight variables has been included for the Confirmatory Factor Analysis (CFA) to test the reliability and validity of variables in the factor. The computed standardized factor loading, its 't' statistics cronbach alpha composite reliability and Average Variance Extracted of the factor are shown in Table 4.23.

The standardized factor loading of the variables in service factor is varying from 0.9102 in free SMS facility to 0.5962 in call waiting facility. The 't' statistics of standardized factor loading of all variables are significant at five per cent level. It reveals the convergent validity of the factor. It is also supported by the composite reliability and Average Variance Extracted since these are greater than 0.5 and 50.00 per cent, respectively. The included eight variables in the 'service' factor explain it to the extent of 84.84 per cent, since its cronbach alpha is 0.8484. Hence, the score of the eight variables are summated to findout the score on the service factor.

Table 4.23: Standardized factor loading of the Variables in Service

Sl. No.	Variables	Standardized Factor loading	t-statistics	Composite Reliability	Average Variance Extracted
1.	Free SMS facility	0.9102	3.9697*	0.8182	58.45
2.	Lesser official formalities	0.8616	3.3081*		
3.	Classification of peak and off-peak hours	0.8233	3.2114*		
4.	Free incoming facility	0.7449	2.9696*		
5.	Higher number of included minutes	0.7069	2.8417*		
6.	Multi-media message facility	0.6817	2.5602*		
7.	Prepaid/post paid facility	0.6236	2.3841*		
8.	Call waiting facility	0.5962	2.0717		
	Cronbach alpha:0.8484.				

*Significant at five per cent level.

Standardized factor loading of the variables in 'Economy' Factor

The Confirmatory Factor Analysis (CFA) has been administered to test the reliability and validity of the six variables included in economy factor. The computed standardized factor loading, its 't' statistics, composite reliability, Average Variance Extracted and Cronbach alpha are given in Table 4.24.

Table 4.24: Standardized factor loading of the Variables in Economy

Sl. No.	Variables	Standardized Factor loading	't' statistics	Composite Reliability	Average Variance Extracted
1.	Low cost SIM card	0.8943	3.7172*	0.7336	52.17
2.	Nominal charges on calls	0.8114	3.3088*		
3.	Reasonable charges on outgoing calls	0.7279	2.9091*		
4.	Low activation charges	0.6086	2.4511*		
5.	Itemized billing	0.5942	2.3216*		
6.	Minimum security amount	0.5316	2.0616*		

Cronbach alpha 0.7336.

*Significant at five per cent level.

The 'economy' factor consists of six variables. The standardized factor loading of the variables in 'economy' factor is varying from 0.8943 in Low cost SIM card to 0.5316 in minimum security amount. The 't' statistics of standardized factor loading of all variables are significant at five per cent level which indicate the convergent validity. It is also confirmed by the composite reliability and Average Variance Extracted. The included six variables in 'Economy' factor explain it to the extent of 73.36 per cent.

Factor loading of the variables in Coverage

The 'Coverage' factor consists of five variables, namely, Network Coverage, Inter Network Coverage, National Roaming Facility, Voice Clarity and good in house coverage, since the factor loading of the variables are higher in the coverage factor compared to other factors. The standardized factor loading of the variables, its 't' statistics and the reliability coefficients are computed to test the reliability and validity of variables in the factor. The CFA has been executed. The results are given in Table 4.25.

Table 4.25: Standardized factor loading of the Variables in Coverage

Sl. No.	Variables	Standardized Factor loading	't' statistics	Composite Reliability	Average Variance Extracted
1.	Network coverage	0.8449	3.4502*	0.7878	54.51
2.	Inter Network coverage	0.7661	2.9193*		
3.	National Roaming facility	0.6908	2.6554*		
4.	Voice Clarity	0.6301	2.2717*		
5.	Good in house coverage	0.5781	2.0142*		
Cronbach alpha 0.8081.					

*Significant at five per cent level.

The included five variables in 'coverage' factor explains it to the extent of 80.81 per cent, since its reliability coefficient is 0.8081. The 't' statistics of the standardized factor loadings of the variables in this factor are significant at five per cent level, which reveals the convergent validity. The composite reliability and Average Variance Extracted by the factor are greater than standardized minimum of 0.5 and 50.00 per cent, respectively. The analysis reveals the reliability and validity of variables in this factor.

Factor loading of the variables in 'Schemes' factors

The four variables related to the scheme are clustered into a factor, since its factor loadings are higher in scheme factor compared to other factors. In order to test the reliability and validity of variables in 'scheme' factor the CFA has been executed. The standardized factor loading of the variables, its 't' statistics, composite reliability and average extracted by the factor are computed and shown in Table 4.26.

The standardized factor loading of the variable is varying from 0.8703 in frequent schemes to 0.5908 in large number of promotional measures. The 't' statistics for the standardized factor loading of all four variables in this factor are significant at five per cent level. It conveys the convergent validity of the factor. It is also supported by the composite reliability and average variance extracted, since these are greater than 0.5 and 50.00 per cent, respectively. The included four variables explain the 'scheme' factor to the extent of 76.63 per cent, since its reliability coefficient is 0.7663.

Table 4.26: Standardized factor loading of the Variables in Schemes

Sl. No.	Variables	Standardized Factor loading	't' statistics	Composite Reliability	Average Variance Extracted
1	Frequent schemes	0.8703	3.3144*	0.7331	51.29
2	Increased validity period	0.6817	2.8182*		
3	Special/festival offer	0.6441	2.3145*		
4	Large number of promotional schemes	0.5908	2.1145*		
Cronbach alpha 0.7663.					

*Significant at five per cent level.

Standardized factor loading of the variables in 'Image'

In total, there are four variables included in the image. The included four variables explain the image factor to the extent of 79.08 per cent. Since its cronbach alpha is 0.7908. The reliability and validity of variables in 'image' have been tested with the help of CFA. The result of CFA is summarized in Table 4.27.

Table 4.27: Standardized factor loading of Variables in Image

Sl. No.	Variables	Standardized Factor loading	't' statistics	Composite Reliability	Average Variance Extracted
1	Frequent schemes	0.8703	3.3144*	0.7331	51.29
1.	Goodwill of the service provider	0.8408	3.1408*	0.7511	53.04
2.	Brand Image	0.7617	2.7816*		
3.	Positive words of mouth	0.6839	2.3144*		
4.	Multi-national company	0.6148	2.0124*		
Cronbach alpha 0.7908.					

*Significant at five per cent level.

The standardized factor loading of the variables is varying from 0.8408 in Goodwill of the service provider to 0.6148 in multi-national company. The 't' statistics of standardized factor loading of all variables in this factor are significant at five per cent level which reveals, the convergent validity. The composite reliability and Average Variance Extracted are greater than their minimum threshold of 0.5 and 50.00 per cent, respectively.

Significant Difference among the Young and Elder Customers in GSM and CDMA Market Regarding their Perception on Factor

In order to exhibit the important factor leading to the service provider among the young and older customers in GSM market, the mean score of all five factors among the two group of customers have been computed separately. In order to find out the significant difference among the two group of customers regarding their perception on factors leading to choice of the service provider, the 't' test has been administered. The resultant mean score of each factor and their respective 't' statistics are shown in Table 4.28.

Table 4.28: Significant difference among the young and elder Customers in GSM market Regarding the Factors

Sl. No.	Factors	Mean score among the customers in		T-statistics
		Youngsters	Elders	
1.	Service	3.0986	3.8922	-1.9681*
2.	Economy	3.7758	3.1690	2.0193*
3.	Coverage	3.2061	3.9842	-2.3863*
4.	Scheme	3.8436	3.1816	2.5403*
5.	Image	3.1611	3.2048	-0.3641

*Significant at five per cent level.

From the Table 4.28, it is shown that the highly viewed factors to choose their service provider among the young customers in GSM market are Scheme and Economy, since the respective mean scores are 3.8436 and 3.7758. Among the elder customers in GSM market, these two factors are coverage and service, since mean scores are 3.9842 and 3.8922, respectively. Regarding the perception on factors leading to choice of the service provider, the significant difference among the two group of customers has been identified in the perception on service, economy, coverage and scheme, since the respective 't' statistics are significant at five per cent level.

Perception on factors among the Customers of various Service Providers

The customers are classified into customers of various service providers, namely, Airtel, Aircel, BSNL, Vodafone, Idea and Others. The mean score of the five factors among the seven group of customers has been computed separately to exhibit the customers' perception on factors. In order to analyse the significant difference among the customers of various service providers regarding their perception on factors, the one way analysis of variance has been administered. The resultant mean score of the factors and the respective 'F' statistics are illustrated in Table 4.29.

Table 4.29 reveals that the most important factors identified by the customers of Airtel and Aircel are service and economy, since the mean scores are 3.9144 and 3.2672, respectively. Among the customers of Vodafone, these two factors are Economy, since the respective mean score is 3.5162. Among the customers of Idea and Others, the important factors are service

Table 4.29: Significant difference among the Customers of various Service Providers

Sl.No.	Factors	Mean Score among the Customers of						F-statistics
		Airtel	Aircel	BSNL	Vodafone	Idea	Others	
1.	Service	3.9144	3.0692	3.2568	3.3441	2.9792	3.0682	3.0844*
2.	Economy	3.4508	3.2672	3.6339	3.5162	2.8081	3.0562	2.9697*
3.	Coverage	3.6817	2.8081	3.9811	3.0671	2.8181	3.1441	3.1443*
4.	Scheme	3.2162	3.1144	3.2696	3.2162	3.4562	3.1441	0.9696
5.	Image	3.4081	2.9092	3.6081	3.0862	2.7339	3.0841	2.6143*

*Significant at five per cent level.

and scheme, since the respective mean scores are 2.9792 and 3.1441. The important factors identified by the customers of BSNL, these are coverage and Economy since the mean scores are 3.9811 and 3.6339. Regarding the perception on factors loading to the service providers, the significant difference among the customers of seven service providers has been identified in the case of perception on service, economy, coverage and Image since the respective 'F' statistics are significant at five per cent level. The analysis indicates that the reasons for choosing the current service provider are different among customers of different service providers.

Association between profile of Customers and their Perception on Factors

The association between the profile of customers and their perception on five factors leading to the service provider have been examined with the help of one way analysis of variance. The included profile variables are sex, age, level of education, occupational background, marital status, family size, personal income number of earning members per family, family income and the personality score of the customers. The resulted 'F' statistics are presented in Table 4.30.

Table 4.30 explains that the perception on 'Service Factor' the significantly associating profile variables are age, level of education and occupational background since the variables regarding the perception on 'economy factor' are sex, age, family size, personal income, number of earning members per family, family income and personality score of the customers. Regarding the perception on 'coverage' factor the significantly associating profile variables are age, occupational background, personal income, number of earning members per family, family income, and personality traits of customers, whereas, regarding the perception on 'Scheme Factor', these profile variables are age, level of education, personal income, number of earning members per family, family income, and personality score of the customers. The significantly associating profile variables regarding perception on 'image factor' are age, level of education, occupational background, personal income, number of earning members

Table 4.30: Association between profile of customers and their Perception on factors leading to Select Service Providers

Sl.No.	Profile Variables	F-Statistics				
		Service	Economy	Coverage	Scheme	Image
1.	Sex	2.2819	3.9197*	1.8684	2.5173	2.3217
2.	Age	2.4578*	2.7076*	2.3962*	3.1718*	2.9088*
3.	Level of Education	2.5676*	2.1173	2.0971	2.5608*	2.2491*
4.	Occupational background	2.3908*	2.0964	2.3631*	2.1446	2.2908*
5.	Marital Status	2.1616	1.8718	1.4064	1.3324	2.1718
6.	Family Size	2.0445	2.5054*	2.1478	1.9897	2.0243
7.	Personal Income	2.4996*	2.3908*	3.1703*	2.5081*	2.4146*
8.	Number of earning members per family	2.5108*	2.7789*	2.9099*	3.1442*	3.6164*
9.	Family Income	2.6817*	2.4508*	2.6787*	3.1142*	3.0963*
10.	Personality Score	2.9845*	3.1403*	2.6787*	3.6069*	3.3969*

*Significant at five per cent level.

per family, family income and personality score of the customers, whereas, regarding the perception on 'scheme factor', these profile variables are age, level of education, personal income number of earning members per family, family income, and personality score of customers. The significantly associating profile variables regarding the perception on 'image factor' are age, level of education, occupational background, personal income, number of earning members per family, family income and personality score since the respective 'F' statistics are significant at five per cent level.

Discriminating factors among the Young and Elder Customers

The young and older Customers in GSM market may differ regarding their perception on factors leading to the choice of the service provider. It is highly imperative to identify the important discriminant factors among the two groups of customers for some policy implications. In order to identify the discriminant factors among the two groups of customers, the two group discriminant analysis has been administered. Initially, the mean difference among the two group of customers has been identified regarding each factor. The Wilk's Lambda of each factor has been examined to find out the discriminant power of each power. The results are illustrated in Table 4.31.

Table 4.31 shows the significant mean difference among the two group of customers has been noticed in the case of service, economy, coverage and scheme, since the respective 't' statistics are significant at five per cent level. The higher mean difference is identified in the case of coverage and scheme factor, since their respective mean differences are -0.4781 and 0.4670. The higher discriminant power of the factor is noticed in the case of economy

Table 4.31: Mean score and discriminant factors leading to choose service provider among the Customers in GSM and CDMA

Sl. No.	Factors	Mean score among on the customers in		Mean Difference	T-Statistics	Wilk's Lambda
		Youngsters	Elders			
1.	Service	3.0986	3.4922	-0.33936	-1.9681*	0.1762
2.	Economy	3.4758	3.1690	0.3068	2.0193*	0.1241
3.	Coverage	3.2061	3.6842	-0.4781	-2.3863*	0.2334
4.	Scheme	3.6486	3.1816	0.4670	2.5403*	0.2437
5.	Image	3.1611	3.2048	-0.0437	-0.3641	0.4869

*Significant at five per cent level.

and service, since the respective Wilk's Lambda coefficients are 0.1241 and 0.1762. Only the significant factors have been included to establish the two group discriminant function. The unstandardized procedure has been followed to establish the function. The estimated discriminant function is :

$$Z = 0.4388 - 0.2471x_1 + 0.3129x_2 + 0.2014x_3 + 0.1611x_4$$

The relative contribution of discriminant factors in total discriminant score is computed by the product of unstandardized canonical discriminant coefficient and the respective mean difference of the factor. The computed relative contribution of discriminant factor in total discriminant score is illustrated in Table 4.32.

Table 4.32: Relative contribution of discriminant factors in Total Discriminant Score

Sl. No.	Factors	Unstandardized Canonical discriminant coefficient	Mean difference	Product	Relative Contribution on Total discriminant score
1.	Service	-0.2471	-0.3936	0.0973	26.68
2.	Economy	0.3129	0.3068	0.0959	26.30
3.	Coverage	0.2014	-0.4781	0.0963	26.40
4.	Scheme	0.1611	0.4670	0.0752	20.62
	Total			**0.3647**	**100.00**
	Per cent of cases correctly classified: 81:42.				

From Table 4.32, it is explained that the higher discriminant coefficient is noticed in economy factor, since the respective discriminant coefficient is 0.3129. It infers that the economy factor influence is more than the discriminant function compared to other factors. The higher relative contribution of discriminant factor in total discriminant score is identified in the case of service, coverage and economy, since the respective constributions are 26.68, 26.41 and 26.30 per cent to the total, respectively. The estimated discriminant function correctly classified the two groups of customers to the extent of 81.42 per cent. The analysis reveals that the important discriminant factors among the two groups of customers are service, and coverage, which are higher among the older customers than the younger customers.

REFERENCES

1. Prahad, C.K. and Ramasamy, V., (2000), "*Co-operating Customer Competencies*" *Harvard Business Review*, January-February, pp.79-87.
2. Yi, Y., (1990), "A Critical review of consumer satisfaction", in Zeithamal, V.A., (Eds.), Review of Marketing, 1990, American Marketing Association, Chicago, IC, pp.68-123.
3. Oliver, R.C., (1981), "Measurement and Evaluation of Satisfaction Powers in Retail Settings", *Journal of Retailing,* 57(Fall), pp.25-48.

Service Quality of the Service Providers and Customers Satisfaction in GSM Market

Introduction

In the past two decades, although more and more research findings have appeared concerning quality, it is still worth noting here that there are several district conceptualizations of quality (Holbrook, 1994)[1]. In Marketing and Economics, quality often has been viewed as dependent on the level of product attributes. In operations management, quality is defined as having two primary dimensions, fitness of use and reliability. In service literature, quality is viewed as an overall assessment (Parasuraman *et al.,* 1988)[2]. Among them, the most comprehensive definition of quality is the one proposed by Garvin (1988)[3] with the following eight attributes:

(*i*) Performance means a product's primary operating characteristics,

(*ii*) Features refer to the additional features of the product,

(*iii*) Conformance represents the extent to which a product's design and operating characteristics meet the established standards,

(*iv*) Reliability indicates the probability that a product will operate properly over a specified period of time under stated conditions of use,

(*v*) Durability means the amount of use the consumer gets from the product before it physically deteriorates or until a replacement is preferable,

(*vi*) Service ability refers to the speed, competence and courtesy of repair,

(*vii*) Aesthetics refer to how a product appeals to the five reuses and

(*viii*) Customers' perceived quality indicates the customers perception of a product's quality, based on the reputation of the Firm.

Service Quality of the Service Provider

Service Sector is quite different from the Manufacturing Sector. It directly deals with the people and involves a large number of transactions and paper work, but very less amount is involved in transaction. There is no formal specification on the quality service required, and so, the scope of making mistakes is more in the Service Sector. It is difficult to quantify the quality in this Sector, as it is less tangible. Moreover, the expectation of the customers is dynamic and is not much strategically oriented and is focussed on a short-term.

The quality of service is decided on the basis of the four major factors in the mobile phone industry; time liners, integrity, predictability and customer satisfaction. The quality of service can be improved using certain approaches like, quality circles, suggestions, schemes, employee empowerment, involvement of top management and commitment, and improved techniques of process. The assessment of customer satisfaction is done on the basis of the service provided.

The service quality of the service providers can be assessed with the help of so many service quality variables. In the present study, the variables are confined to thirty one variables. The variables related to the service quality in mobile phone service are derived from the reviews (Prahad and Ramasamy, 2000[4]; Wang and Hing, (2002)[5]; and Leisen and Vance, (2001)[6]; these are listed in Table 5.1.

The customers are asked to rate the above-said thirty one variables at five point scale according to customers' expectation and perception separately. The customers' expectation is measured from highly expected to not at all expected, which carries the score from 5 to 1,. respectively. The customers' perception is measured at five point scale from highly satisfied to highly dissatisfied which carries the marks from 5 to 1, respectively. The data related to the score on expectation and perception has been included for the analysis.

The reliability and validity measurement scale for the service quality of mobile service is conducted with the help of convergent validity. The convergent validity of a construct could be proven only if the following criterion is verified: when the construct of perceived service quality in mobile phone service sector is measured by two different instruments, both measures must converge. (Peter, 1981)[7]. Therefore, to test the convergent validity of service quality by expectation and perception, the study analysed the association between the service quality scores on expectation and perception. The association between these two scores was analyzed with a one way analysis of variance. This association was statistically significant at five per cent level (F=36.6033; P=.0000). This reflects a good convergent validity for service quality in mobile phone industry by expectation and perception.

Table 5.1: Variables in Service Quality of the Service Providers

Sl.No.	Variables in Service Quality
1.	Providing service as promised
2.	Connecting call easily
3.	Telling customer exactly what services will be performed
4.	Employees instill confidence in customers
5.	Speedy delivery of SMS
6.	Getting news, Jokes and others
7.	Electronic recharging
8.	Sincere in solving the problems
9.	Facility of getting missed call
10.	Recharging without hassles through easy deal
11.	Providing prompt service to customers
12.	Getting booster exchange
13.	Performing service right at the first time
14.	Easy recharging
15.	Neat and knowledgeable employees
16.	Various options in recharging coupons
17.	Immediate Customer care
18.	No problems in setting calls
19.	Providing service at the promised time
20.	Recharge facilities
21.	Customers feel comfortable interacting with employees
22.	Song options for dialer times
23.	Modernization of networks
24.	Voice clarity Net works
25.	Employees are consistent
26.	Quick activation of number
27.	Frequent schemes
28.	Maintain error-free-records
29.	Employees are trust worthy
30.	Willing to help customers
31.	Always ready to respond to customers request

Service Quality Factors in Mobile Phone Service Market

The service quality factors in the mobile phone service market are drawn from the score on the service quality of mobile phone providers with the help of factor analysis. Before conducting the factor analysis, the validity of data for factor analysis has been examined with the help KMO measure of sampling adequacy and the Barkletts test of sphericity. The KMO measures of sampling adequacy (0.7929) satisfies the validity of data for factor analysis, which is also confirmed by the zero per cent level of significance of Chi-Square value. The executed factor analysis results in six important service quality factors, namely, basic services, value added services, customer care, responsiveness, assurance and recharge. The service quality variables included in each service quality factors, its reliability, eigen value and per cent of variation explained by the factor are summarized in Table 5.2.

Table 5.2: Service quality factors in GSM Market

Sl. No.	Service Quality factors	Number of variables included	Eigen Value	Per cent of variation explained	Reliability Coefficient
1.	Basic services	6	4.1314	21.08	0.7408
2.	Value added services	5	3.6807	17.17	0.8249
3.	Customer care	5	2.9691	15.26	0.7911
4.	Responsiveness	5	2.5083	13.37	0.7647
5.	Assurance	5	1.9884	10.08	0.8616
6.	Recharge	5	1.2162	8.17	0.7339
	Total	31		85.13	
	KMO measure of sampling Adequacy: 0.7929		Bartletts test of sphericity; Chi-square value: 87.08*		

*Significant at zero per cent level.

Table 5.2 explains that, the thirty one service quality variables are narrated into six service quality factors that explain the service quality variables to the extent of 85.13 per cent. The important service quality factors identified by the factor analysis quality are basic services, value added services and customer care since, its eigen values are 4.1314, 3.6807 and 2.9691, respectively. The other three service quality factors are responsiveness, assurance and recharge with the eigen value of 2.5083, 1.9884 and 1.2162, respectively. The per cent of variation explained by the first three factors are 21.08, 17.17 and 15.26 per cent respectively, whereas, by the last three factors, are 13.37, 10.08 and 8.17 per cent, respectively.

Standardized factors loading of the variables in 'Basic Service' Factor

The service quality variables related to the quality of basic service among the service providers are clustered into one factor, and hence it is named as Basic Services. This factor consists of six variables, namely, quick activation of number, connecting calls easily, no problems in getting calls, speedy delivering of SMS, voice clarity of network and recharge facilities.

In order to test the reliability and validity of the six variables in Basic Service, the Confirmatory, Factor Analysis (CFA) have been executed. The standardized factor loading of the variables, its 't' statistics, composite reliability and Average Variance extracted by the factor are summarized in Table 5.3.

Table 5.3: Standardized factor loading of Variables in Basic Services

Sl. No.	Variables	Standardized Factor loading	't' statistics	Composite reliability	Average Variance Extracted
1.	Quick activation of Number	0.8344	3.2442		51.29
2.	Connecting calls easily	0.7247	2.5161*	0.7129	
3.	No problems in getting calls	0.7069	2.4033*		
4.	Speedy delivery of SMS	0.6891	2.3646*		
5.	Voice clarity Network	0.6403	2.2141*		
6.	Recharge facilities	0.5962	2.0042*		
	Cronbach alpha: 0.7408				

*Significant at five per cent level.

The standardized factor loading of the variables in Basic Factor is varying from 0.8344 in Quick activation of Number to 0.5962 in recharge facilities. The 't' statistics of the standardized factor loading of all variables are significant at five per cent level, which reveals the convergent validity of the Factor. It is also supported by the composite reliability and Average variance extracted, since these are greater than the minimum threshold of 0.5 and 50.00 per cent respectively. The included six variables in this factor explain it to the extent of 74.08 per cent, since its reliability coefficient is 0.7408. Hence, the analysis conclude that the six variables have been included to represent the 'Basic Service' Factor in variable.

Standardized factor loading of the variables in 'Value Added Services' Factor

The 'value added services' factor consists of five variable, namely, song options for dialer; facility of getting missed call details; getting news, jokes and others; getting booster recharge; and modernization of net works, since their respective factor loadings are higher in the tangibility factor than in other factors. The CFA has been administered to findout the reliability and validity of the variables in 'value-added services' factor. The computed standardized factor loading, its 't' statistics, composite reliability, Average variance extracted and cron bach alpha are summarized in Table 5.4.

The included five variables in the 'value added services' factor explain it to the extent of 82.44 per cent, since its cronbach alpha is 0.8249. The 't' statistics of the standardized factor loading of all variables in this Factor are significant at five per cent level, which reveals the convergent validity. The composite reliability and Average Variance Extracted are greater than its standard minimum of 0.5 and 50.00 per cent, respectively. The analysis

Table 5.4: Standardized factor loading of variables in 'value added' Services Factor

Sl. No.	Variables	Standardized Factor loading	't' statistics	Composite reliability	Average Variance Extracted
1.	Song options for dialer	0.9147	4.1039*	0.8011	59.17
2.	Facility of getting missed	0.8307	3.2791*		
3.	Getting news, jokes & others	0.7396	2.5072*		
4.	Getting booster recharge	0.6817	3.4033*		
5.	Modernization of Networks	0.6207	3.3011*		
	Cronbach alpha 0.8249.				

*Significant at five per cent level

reveals the reliability and validity of the variables included in the 'value added services' Factor.

Standardized factor Loading of the Variables in Customer Care

Since the variables, namely, performing since right the from first time, maintain error-free records, providing service as promised, providing service at the promised time and sincerity in solving the problem have the higher factor loading with this Factor, it is clustered and named as 'customer care' factor. The standardized factor loading of the variables, its 't' statistics, composite reliability and average variance extracted by the factor are computed with the help of CFA in order to test the reliability and validity of variables in this Factor. The result of CFA is given in Table 5.5.

Table 5.5: Standardised factor loading of variables in 'customer care'

Sl. No.	Variables	Standardized Factor loading	't' statistics	Composite reliability	Average Variance Extracted
1.	Performing right since the first time	0.8911	3.9402*	0.745	52.03
2.	Maintain error-free records	0.7908	2.9909*		
3.	Providing service as promised	0.6869	2.4544*		
4.	Providing service at the promised time	0.6217	2.2042*		
5.	Sincere in solving the problem	0.5803	1.9969*		
	Cronbach alpha: 0.7911.				

*Significant at five per cent level.

From Table 5.5, it is inferred that the included five variables in 'customer care' factor explain it to the extent of 79.11 per cent, since its reliability coefficient is 0.7911. The standardized factor loading of the variables is varying from 0.8911 in performing right since the first time to 0.5803 in service in solving the problem. The 't' statistics of standardized factor loading of the variables are significant five per cent level which reveals the convergent validity. It is also supported by the composite reliability and Average Variance Extracted, since these are greater than 0.50 and 50.00 per cent, respectively. The analysis reveals that the included five variable in 'customer care' factor explains it to a reasonable extent.

Standardized factor loading of the variables in 'responsiveness' factor

The responsiveness factor consists of five variables, namely, willingness to help customers, telling customers exactly what service will be provided, always ready to respond to customers' request, immediate customer care and providing prompt service to customers, since their respective factor loadings are higher in this Factor compared to other Factors. The CFA has been executed to test the validity and reliability of the variables in 'responsiveness' Factor. The result of CFA is given in Table 5.6.

Table 5.6: Standardized Factor loading of Variables in Responsiveness

Sl. No.	Variables	Standardized Factor loading	't' statistics	Composite reliability	Average Variance Extracted
1.	Willingness to help customers	0.8442	3.4082*	0.7244	52.11
2.	Telling customers exactly what services will be provided	0.7917	3.0911*		
3.	Always ready to respond to customers request	0.7303	2.7082*		
4.	Immediate customers care	0.6917	2.6146*		
5.	Providing Prompt service to customers	0.6211	2.3039*		
Cronbach alpha: 0.7647.					

*Significant at five per cent level.

From Table 5.5, it is inferred that the standardized Factor loading of the variables is varying from 0.8442 willingness to help customers to 0.6211 in providing prompt service to customer. The 't' statistics of standardized factor loading of the variables are significant at five per cent level, which indicates the convergent validity of the Factor. The composite reliability and Average Variance Extracted are greater than its standard minimum of 0.50 and 50.00 per cent respectively, which also support the convergent validity. The included five variables in this Factor explain it to the extent of 76.47 per cent, since its reliability coefficient is 0.7647. The analysis infers that the included five variables in responsiveness are representing it to a reliable extent.

Standardized factor loading of the variables in the 'assurance' factor

The variables, namely, employees are consistently courteous, customers feel comfortable with employees, employees instill confidence in customers, employees are trustworthy and neat and knowledgeable employees have more Factor loading with the assurance Factor, hence it is called as 'assurance factor'. The Confirmatory Factor Analysis (CFA) has been executed to test the reliability and validity of the variables in this Factor. The result of CFA is illustrated in Table 5.7.

Table 5.7: Standardized factor loading of variables in Assurance Factor

Sl. No.	Variables	Standardized Factor loading	't' statistics	Composite reliability	Average Variance Extracted
1.	Employees are consistently courteous	0.9317	4.1108*	0.8232	56.73
2.	Customers feel comfortable interacting with employees	0.8608	3.5869*		
3.	Employees in still confidence in customers	0.7811	2.9099*		
4.	Employees are trustworthy	0.7308	2.5145*		
5.	Neat and knowledgeable employees	0.6561	2.2165*		
Cronbach alpha: 0.8616.					

*Significant at five per cent level.

The included five variables in the 'assurance' Factor explain it to the extent of 86.16 per cent, since its reliability coefficient is 0.8616. The standardized factor loading of the variables in this Factor varying from 0.9317 in 'employees are consistently courteous' to 0.6561 in 'Neat and knowledgeable employees'. It indicates the convergent validity of the Factor. It is also supported by the composite reliability and Average Variance Extracted by the Factor, since these are greater than 0.5 and 50.00 per cent, respectively. The analysis justify the summation of the score of the variables are representing the score on 'assurance' among the customers to a reliable extent.

Factor loading of the variable in 'recharging' factor

The empathy Factor consists of five variables, namely, Electronic recharging, various options in recharging coupons, recharging without hassels through easy deal, frequent schemes and easy recharging, since the respective Factor loadings are higher in this Factor than in other Factors. The standardize Factor loading of the variables and 't' statistics have been computed with the help of CFA in order to analyse the reliability and validity of variables in this Factor. The result of CFA is presented in Table 5.8.

Table 5.8: Standardized factor loading of variables in 'recharge' factor

Sl. No.	Variables	Standardized Factor loading	't' statistics	Composite reliability	Average Variance Extracted
1.	'E' recharging	0.8147	3.3392*	0.7339	52.75
2.	Various options in recharging coupons	0.7302	3.1045*		
3.	Recharging with out hassels through easy deal	0.6916	2.9709*		
4.	Frequent schemes	0.6108	2.1144*		
5.	Easy recharging	0.5962	2.0646*		
Cronbach alpha: 0.7339.					

*Significant at five per cent level.

The included five variables in the 'Recharge' Factor explain it to the extent of 73.39 per cent, since their respective reliability coefficient is 0.7339. The 't' statistics for the standardized Factor loading of the variables are significant at five per cent level, which reveals the convergent validity. It is also supported by the composite reliability and Average variance extracted, since their respective values are greater than their minimum threshold of 0.5 and 50.00 per cent, respectively. The analysis reveals that the five variables in 'Recharge' explain it to a reliable extent.

Perception and Expectation on Service Quality Factors among the Customers

The perception score on six service quality Factors is derived from the mean score of the perception on various service quality variables in each service quality Factor. Similarly, the score of expectation on the service quality factors is drawn from the mean score of expectation on six service quality Factors among the young and older customers in GSM Market. The mean scores are computed separately to exhibit the level of perception and expectation on service quality Factors. The results are given in Table 5.9.

Table 5.9: Mean of perception and expectation on service quality factors among the young and elder customers

Sl.No.	Service quality	Mean Score among the Customers in			
		Youngster		Elders	
		Perception	Expectation	Perception	Expectation
1.	Basic Services	3.6186	3.9384	2.9181	3.5687
2.	Value added Services	2.8608	3.3091	3.8086	3.6808
3.	Customer care	3.7183	3.9103	2.8693	3.8713
4.	Responsiveness	3.8684	3.8517	3.0143	3.6861
5.	Assurance	3.5681	3.7086	2.7181	3.7233
6.	Recharge	3.8083	3.9184	3.0144	3.8244

*Significant at five per cent level.

The higher perception on service quality Factors among the young customers in GSM Market is identified in responsiveness and recharge since the mean scores are 3.8684 and 3.8083, respectively, whereas, among the older customers in GSM Market, these two service quality Factors are value added services and recharge. At the same time, the mean of expectation among the young customers in GSM is noticed in the case of Basic of Services and recharge, since the perspective mean scores are 3.9384 and 3.9184, whereas, among the elder customers in GSM, these two are customer care and recharge, since the mean scores are 3.8713 and 3.8244, respectively.

Service Quality Gap among the Customers in GSM Market

The service quality gap indicates the difference between the perception and expectation on various service quality factors. The negative values indicate that there is less perception on service quality factor compared to respective expectation. The customers in GSM Market are classified into customers of Airtel, Aircel, Vodafone, BSNL, Idea and others. The service quality gap on quality of service, tangibility, reliability, responsiveness, assurance and empathy have been computed separately among the customers of different service providers. The one way analysis of variance has been executed to significant difference among the four groups of customers regarding their service quality gaps.

Table 5.10: Service quality gap among the customers in GSM

Sl.No.	Service Quality Factors	Mean score among the customers in						F-statistics
		Airtel	Aircel	BSNL	Vodafone	Idea	Others	
1.	Basic services	-.2934	-.3997	-.4576	-.2865	-.5868	-.4412	2.9698*
2.	Value added services	-.2042	-.4568	-.6862	-.5199	-.3996	-.2909	3.0141*
3.	Customers care	-.1021	-.2192	-.2111	-.1962	-.2085	-.3016	2.3107*
4.	Responsiveness	.0968	-.1192	-.0867	.1234	-.1227	-.2011	2.4096*
5.	Assurance	-.1219	-.2093	-.1268	-.1335	-.1668	-.1773	2.8187*
6.	Recharge	-.0841	-.1968	-.1468	-.1142	-.1902	-.1406	2.2669*

*Significant at five per cent level.

Table 5.10 indicates that all service gaps are in the negative, except a single case. Among the customers of Airtel, the negative service quality gaps are identified as high in quality of basic service and value added services, since their respective service quality gaps are –0.2934 and –0.2042. Among the customers of Aircel, these are valued added services and basic services, since the respective mean score on service quality gaps are -0.4568 and 0.3997, respectively. The higher service quality gap among the customers in Vodafone is noticed in the case of value added services and quality of basic services, since its means scores are -0.5199 and -0.2845, respectively. Regarding the BSNL customers, the higher service quality gaps are identified in the case of value added service and basic services, since their respective mean of service quality gaps are -0.6862 and -0.4576, respectively. Regarding the customers of Idea, the higher service quality gap is noticed in the case of basic services and value added services, since their respective mean scores are -0.5868 and 0.3996. Among the Others customers, these service quality Factors are basic services and customer care, since their respective mean of service quality gaps are -0.4412 and -0.3016. Regarding the service quality gap, the significant difference among the customers of various service providers have been identified in all service quality factors, since the respective 'F' statistics are significant at five per cent level.

Discriminant Service Quality Gap Among the Young and Elder Customers in GSM Market

The service quality gap is in the negative on many service quality Factors, except one or two. The service quality gap among the two groups of customers may differ from each other. It is highly imperative to identify the important discriminant service quality gap among the two groups of customers for some policy implications. The mean difference in each service quality gap among the two group of customers, its statistical significance and the Wilks' Lambda coefficients are compared to exhibit the discriminant power of the service quality gap. The results are shown in Table 5.11.

Table 5.11: Mean difference and discriminant power of service quality gap among young and elder customers in GSM market

Sl. No.	Service Quality Gap	Mean Score among customers in		Mean Difference	T-statistics	Wilks' Lambda
		Youngster	Elders			
1.	Basic service gap	-.3198	-.6506	.3308	1.9962*	0.4563
2.	Value added service gap	-.4483	.1278	.5761	2.1718*	0.3917
3.	Customers care gap	-.1920	-1.0020	.8100	3.2165*	0.1608
4.	Responsiveness gap	.0167	-0.6718	.6885	2.5086*	0.3067
5.	Assurance gap	-.1405	-.0052	0.8647	3.9684*	0.1304
6.	Recharge gap	-.1101	-0.8100	.6999	3.0617*	0.2143

*Significant at five per cent level.

The significant mean difference is identified in all service quality gap among the two groups of customers. The higher mean difference is noticed in the case of assurance gap and customer care gap, since the respective mean differences are 0.8647 and 0.8100. The higher discriminant power is identified in the case of assurance gap and customer care gap, since the respective Wilks' Lambda coefficients are 0.1304 and 0.1608. The significant service gaps are included for the establishment of two discriminant analysis. The unstandardized procedure has been followed to establish the function.

$$Z = 0.5149 + 0.2864x_1 + 0.091x_2 + 0.1336x_3 + 0{,}1068x_4 + 0.1144x_5 + 0{,}1036x_6$$

The relative contribution of discriminant service quality gap in the total discriminant score is computed by the product of unstandardized canonical discriminant coefficient and the respective mean difference of the service quality gap. The resultant discriminant coefficient of the service quality gaps and the relative contribution of service quality gaps in total discriminant score are summarized in Table 5.12.

Table 5.12: Relative Contribution of service quality gap in Total Discriminant Score

Sl. No.	Service Quality Gap	Unstandardized canonical discriminant coefficient	Mean difference	Product	Relative contribution in Total discriminant score
1.	Basic service gap	.2864	.3308	0.0947	18.93
2.	Value added service	.0911	.5761	0.0525	10.49
3.	Customer care	.1336	.8100	.1082	21.63
4.	Responsiveness gap	.1068	.6885	.0735	14.69
5.	Assurance gap	.1144	.8647	.0989	19.77
6.	Recharge gap	.1036	.6999	.0725	14.49
	Total			.5003	100.00
	Per cent of cases correctly classified: 78.04.				

Table 5.12 explains that the higher discriminant coefficient is noticed in the case of Basic of service gap, Customer care gap and Assurance gap. Since the respective discriminant coefficients are 0.2864, 0.1336 and 0.1144. It infers the degree of influence of the above said service quality gap in discriminating the two group of customers in GSM Market. The higher relative contribution in total discriminant score is noticed in the case of Customer gap and Assurance gap, since the relative contributions are 21.63 and 19.77 per cent to the total respectively. The per cent of cases correctly classified by the established discriminant function is to the extent of 78.04 per cent. The analysis reveals that the important discriminant service quality gap among the two group of customers in GSM Market are Customers care and Assurance gap, whereas, these two are very high among older customers than the young customers. Since the olders' perception on the customer care and assurance factor is comparatively very less with respective to their level of expectations and also the level of perception on young customers.

Association between the Profile of the Customers and their Service Quality Gap

The profile of the customer may play its own role in expectation and perception on the service quality of mobile phone services. Hence the present study has made an attempt on analyzing the association between the profile of customers and their service quality gap. The included profile variables are sex, age, level of education, occupational background, marital status, family size, personal income, Number of caring members per family, family income and personality score. The association between the profile of customers with each service quality gap is assessed with the help of one way analysis of variance. The resulted 'F' statistics are given in Table 5.13.

Table 5.13: Association between profile of customers and their Service Quality Gap

Sl. No.	Profile Variables	F-statistics					
		Basic service gap	Valued added service gap	Customer care gap	Responsive-ness gap	Assurance gap	Recharge gap
1.	Gender	3.0317	2.4547	2.9103	3.2719	3.1917	2.7193
2.	Age	2.5068*	2.4018*	2.6169*	2.2108*	2.4508*	1.8609
3.	Level of Education	2.6869*	1.7917	2.4508*	2.7192*	2.5617*	2.0623
4.	Occupational background	2.4063*	2.6334*	1.8089	2.0144	2.6083*	2.4094*
5.	Marital status	1.9183	2.0144	2.4093*	2.5092*	1.6933	2.4429*
6.	Family size	2.4037*	2.6029*	2.5132*	1.9963	2.5174*	2.1034
7.	Personal Income	2.3991*	2.5084*	2.6069*	2.8221*	2.6033*	2.8182*
8.	Number of caring members per family	2.7684*	2.7112*	3.0865*	2.9021*	3.7085*	3.3314*
9.	Family Income	2.4604*	3.1145*	2.7108*	2.7086*	2.9183*	3.0624*
10.	Personality Score	2.8616*	3.0141*	4.2245*	3.6556*	2.9185*	3.2041*

*Significant at five per cent level.

Table 5.13 concludes that regarding the perception on the Basic service gap, the significantly associating profile variables are age, level of education, occupational background, family size, personal income, number of caring members per family, family income and personality score, since the respective 'F' statistics are significant at five per cent level. The significantly associating profile variables regarding the perception on value added services gap are age, occupational background, family size, personal income and number of caring members per family, family income and personality score among the customers, whereas, regarding the reliability gap, these profile variables are age, level of education, martial status, family size, personal income, number of caring members per family, family income and personality score. Regarding the perception on responsiveness gap, the significantly associating profile variables are level of education, martial status, personal income number of caring, members per family, family income and personality score of the customers. While in the perception on Recharge gap, these profile variables are occupational background, marital status, personal income, number of caring members per family, family income and personality score of the customers.

Overall Attitude Towards the Service Offered in GSM Market

Customer satisfaction has long been recognized in marketing thought and practices as a central concept as well as an important goal of all business activities (Anderson *et al.*, 1994; Yi 1990)[8]. Consumer satisfaction has different levels of specificity in various studies. Although satisfaction with, a say, a product attribute (Bettman, 1974)[9], a sales person (Swan and Oliver, 1977)[10], and a consumption experience (Bearden and Teel, 1983[11]; Oliver, 1981[12]), may be useful, a more fundamental level is, and should be the satisfaction with a commodity or service. In fact, there are at least two different conceptualizations of customer satisfaction, one is, transaction-specific, the other is cumulative (Anderson, 2000)[13]. From a transaction specific perspective, customer satisfaction is viewed as a post-choice evaluative judgement of specific percentage occasion (Oliver, 1993)[14]. There exists relationship between service quality and customer satisfaction (Sullivan, 1993)[15].

The variables related to the management of overall attitude towards service providers is given in Table 5.20.

Table 5.14: Variables in overall attitude towards the Service Providers

Sl. No.	Variables
1.	Activation formalities
2.	Call charges
3.	Plan options
4.	Clarity of signals
5.	Service quality
6.	Product quality
7.	Connectivity
8.	Basic services
9.	Value added services
10.	Coverage of network
11.	Voice clarity

The customers are asked to rate the overall service offered by the service providers in GSM Market at five point scale, namely, highly satisfied, satisfied, moderate, dissatisfied and highly dissatisfied. The assigned scores on these scales are from 5 to 1, respectively. The mean score of the variables in overall attitude towards service providers among the young and older customers have been computed separately. The results are given in Table 5.15.

The highly perceived variables among the young customers are voice clarity and plan options, since their respective mean scores are 3.9024 and 3.8996 respectively. Among the older customers, these are clarity of signals and coverage of the network, since its mean scores are 3.8641 and 3.2565, respectively. Regarding the perception on the variables, the significant difference among the young and older customer has been noticed in the case of plan options, service quality, basic services, value added services, coverage of the network, and voice clarity, since their respective 't' statistics are significant at five per cent level. The overall perception is higher among the youngsters than the elders.

Table 5.15: Mean score of the variables in overall attitude towards the Service Provide

Sl. No.	Variables	Mean score among customers in		T-statistics
		Youngsters	Elders	
1.	Activation formalities	3.4546	3.0145	1.2452
2.	Call changes	3.5802	3.1123	1.1996
3.	Plan options	3.8996	3.0344	2.7884*
4.	Clarity of signals	3.7075	3.8641	-0.2449
5.	Service quality	3.8145	3.1045	2.5646*
6.	Product quality	3.5691	3.0241	1.3344
7.	Connectivity	3.7723	3.2546	1.6529
8.	Basic services	3.8245	3.1408	2.8024*
9.	Value added services	3.7909	3.0411	2.6557*
10.	Coverage of the network	3.8508	3.2565	2.0451*
11.	Voice clarity	3.9024	3.1456	2.7374*

*Significant at five per cent level.

Reliability and Validity of Variables in Overall Attitude

In total, 11 variables are included to measure the overall attitude towards the service provider. It is imperative to analyse the reliability and validity of variables included in overall attitude. The Confirmatory Factor Analysis (CFA) has been executed to analyse it. The score of the eleven variables in overall attitude has been included for the analysis. The result of CFA is given in Table 5.16.

The included 11 variables explain the overall attitude towards service provider to the extent of 81.28 per cent, since its reliability coefficient is 0.8728. The 't' statistics of the standardized factor loading of the variables are significant at five per cent level, which reveals the convergent validity of the construct. It is also supported by the composite validity and Average Variance Extracted, since their respective values are greater than their minimum threshold of 0.5 and 50.00 per cent, respectively. The analysis concludes that the variables included in the overall attitude towards service provider explain it to a reliable extent.

Table 5.16: Standardized Factor loading of the Variables in Overall Attitude

Sl. No.	Variables	Standardized factor loading	t-statistics	Composite reliability	Average Variance Extracted
1.	Connectivity	0.9144	4.3544*	0.8107	58.02
2.	Service quality	0.8943	3.9694*		
3.	Plan options	0.7682	3.1403*		
4.	Value added services	0.7239	2.9907*		
5.	Activation formalities	0.7065	2.8514*		
6.	Basic services	0.6843	2.5865*		
7.	Coverage network	0.6211	2.4148*		
8.	Call changes	0.6085	2.3341*		
9.	Product quality	0.5911	2.2969*		
10.	Clarity of signals	0.5865	2.0562*		
11.	Voice clarity	0.5733	1.9992*		
	Cronbach alpha : 0.8128.				

Overall Attitude Score (OAS) among the Customers

The overall attitude score towards the service provider among the customers has been measured with the help of the mean score of the variables in the overall attitude. The OAS in the present Study is confined to less than 2.0, 2.0 to 3.00; 3.01 to 4.00 and above 4.00. The distribution of customers on the basis of OAS is illustrated in Table 5.17.

Table 5.17: Overall Attitude Score among the Customers

Sl.No.	OAS	Number of customers in		
		Youngsters	Elders	Total
1.	Less than 2.0	42	64	106
2.	2.0-3.00	68	85	153
3.	3.01-4.00	186	97	283
4.	Above 4.0	117	34	151
	Total	**413**	**280**	**693**

Source: Primary data.

The important OAS among the customers is 3.01 to 4.00 and 2.00 to 3.00, which constitutes 40.84 and 22.08 per cent to the total, respectively. The customers with the OAS constitutes 21.79 per cent to the total. The important OAS among the youngsters 3.01 to 4.00 and above 4.00, which constitutes 45.03 and 28.33 per cent to its total respectively. Among the older customers, the important OAS is 3.01 to 4.00 and 2.00 to 3.00 which constitutes 34.64 and 30.36 per cent to its total, respectively. The analysis reveals that the OAS among the young customers are greater than the older customers.

Overall Attitude among Customers of Various Service Providers

The overall attitude towards the service provider among the customers of different service providers, namely, Airtel, Aircel, BSNL, Vodafone, Idea and Others has been computed separately in order to exhibit the customers' overall attitude. The one way analysis of variance has been executed to analyse the significant difference among the customers of various service providers regarding their overall attitude. The results are given in Table 5.18.

Table 5.18: Overall Attitude score among the Customers of various Service Providers

Sl. No.	Service provider	Mean	Standard deviation	Coefficient of variation in per cent
1.	Airtel	3.5054	0.8142	23.22
2.	Aircel	3.4132	0.6089	17.84
3.	BSNL	3.7758	0.5144	13.62
4.	Vodafone	2.8185	0.5902	20.94
5.	Idea	3.9029	0.8145	20.87
6.	Others	3.7145	0.9244	24.88
	F-statistics	8.1486*		

Source: Primary data.
*Significant at five per cent level.

The higher level of perception has been noticed among the customers of Idea, since its mean score is 3.9029. It is followed by the customers of BSNL and Others, since their respective mean scores are 3.7758 and 3.7145. The higher consistency in the overall attitude score is identified among the customers of BSNL and Aircel since their respective coefficient of variations are 13.62 and 17.84 per cent. Regarding the overall attitude, the significant difference among the customers of various service providers has been identified since their respective 'F' statistics are significant at five per cent level.

Association between the Profile of the Customers and their OAS

Since the profile of the customers may be associated with the overall attitude score among the customers, the present Study has made an attempt to analyse the association with the help of one way analysis of variance. The included profile variables are gender, age, level of education, occupational background, marital status, family size, personal income, number of earning members per family, family income and the personality score of the customers. The results are given in Table 5.19.

Table 5.19: Association between Profile of Customers and their OAS

Sl. No.	Profile variables	F-statistics	Table value of 'F' at five per cent level	Result
1.	Gender	2.9984	3.84	Insignificant
2.	Age	2.8508	2.37	Significant
3.	Level of education	2.7766	2.21	Significant
4.	Occupational background	2.0517	2.37	Insignificant
5.	Marital status	2.1142	2.37	Insignificant
6.	Family size	1.2914	2.37	Insignificant
7.	Personal income	3.1447	2.37	Insignificant
8.	Number of earning members per family	2.8445	2.60	Significant
9.	Family income	3.2446	2.60	Significant
10.	Personality score	3.8048	2.60	Significant

The significantly associating profile variables with the overall attitude towards their service providers among the customers are their age, level of education, personal income, number of earning member per family, family income and personality score, since their respective 'F' statistics are significant at five per cent level. The analysis indicates the importance of above-said profile variables in the overall attitude towards the service provider among the customers.

Expectation on Service Quality Factors among the Customers

The level of expectation on SQFs among the customers are computed by the mean score of expectation on various variables in all SQFs. It is computed among the customers of Airtel, Aircel, BSNL, Vodafone, Idea and Others separately to exhibit their customers' expectations on SQFs. The one way analysis of variance has been executed to analyse the significant difference among the customers of various service providers regarding their level of expectation on SQFs. The mean, standard deviation and coefficient of variation on the level of expectation on SQFs among the customers is given in Table 3.20.

The customers of Idea and Vodafone are expecting more service quality compared to the customers of other service providers, since their respective mean scores are 4.1113, 3.9512, and 3.9481. The higher consistency in the level of expectation is found among the customers of Vodafone. Since, the 'F' statistics are significant at five per cent level, the analysis infers that there is a significant difference among the six group of customers regarding their level of expectation on SQFs altogether.

Table 5.20: Expectation on SQFs among Customers of various Service Providers

Sl. No.	Service providers	Mean	Standard deviation	Coefficient of variation
1.	Airtel	3.8046	0.5645	14.84
2.	Aircel	3.4856	0.6217	17.84
3.	BSNL	3.3069	0.9086	27.48
4.	Vodafone	3.9481	0.3884	9.74
5.	Idea	4.1113	0.4291	10.44
6.	Others	3.9512	0.4108	10.39

F-statistics 6.4245*

*Significant at five per cent level.

Discriminant Expectation of SQFS Among the Satisfaction and Dissatisfaction

The level of expectation on SQFs among the satisfaction and dissatisfaction may be different. Infact, the higher level of expectation on SQFs may lead to more service quality gap among the customers. Hence, the present Study has made an attempt to identify the important discriminant SQFs among the two group of customers regarding their level of expectation. The customers with the OAS above 4.00 is treated as satisfaction, whereas, below 2.0 is treated as dissatisfaction in the present Study. The number of customers in these two categories are respectively. Initially, the mean difference among the two group of customers, its 't' statistics and discriminant power of the SQFs have been computed and illustrated in Table 5.21.

Table 5.21: Mean difference and Discriminant power of SQFs among Satisfies and Disasters (Expectation)

Sl. No.	SQFs	Mean score among		Mean Difference	't' statistics	Wilks Lambda
		Satisfies	Dissatisfies			
1.	Basic services (X_1)	3.3845	3.9815	-0.5970	-2.3345*	-.1323
2.	Value added services (X_2)	3.2456	3.9386	-0.6930	-2.8844*	0.1041
3.	Customer care (X_3)	3.3088	3.9917	-0.6829	-2.7217*	0.1224
4.	Responsiveness (X_4)	3.5063	3.9091	-0.4028	-1.8546	0.2668
5.	Assurance (X_5)	3.6961	3.9033	-0.2123	-0.8561	0.3445
6.	Recharge (X_6)	3.6085	3.9545	-0.3460	-1.2144	0.3217

*Significant at five per cent level.

The significant mean difference among the 'satisfies' and 'dissatisfies' has been noticed in their level of expectation on basic services, values added services and customer care, since their respective 't' statistics are significant at five per cent level. The higher mean difference is noticed in the case of value added service and customer care, since their mean differences are -

0.6930 and -0.6829, respectively. The higher discriminant power of SQF is identified in the case of value added services and customer care, since its wilks Lambda are 0.1041 and 0.1224, respectively. The significant SQFs have been included for the establishment of two group discriminant functions. The unstandardized procedure have been followed to estimate the functions. The estimated discriminant function is:

$$Z = -0.9909 - 0.2452x_1 - 0.4573x_2 - 0.5844x_3$$

The relative contribution of the SQFs in TDS is computed by the product of discriminant coefficient and the mean difference of the respective SQFs. The results are given in Table 5.22.

Table 5.22: Relative Contribution of Discriminant SQFs in TQS

Sl. No.	SQFs	Discriminant coefficient	Mean Difference	Product	Relative contribution in TDS
1.	Basic services	-0.2452	-0.5970	0.1464	16.97
2.	Valued added services	-0.4573	-0.6930	0.3169	36.75
3.	Customer care	-0.5844	-0.6829	0.3991	46.28
	Total			0.8624	100.00
	Per cent of cases correctly classified: 69.04.				

The higher discriminant coefficients are identified in the case of customer care and value added service, since their discriminant coefficients are -0.5844 and –0.4573, respectively. It shows that the above said two SQFs have more influence in the discriminant function. The higher relative contribution of SQFs in TDS have been identified in the case of customer care and value added services since their relative contributions are 46.28 and 36.75, respectively. The estimated discriminant function correctly classifies the 'satisfies' and 'dissatisfies' to the extent of 69.04 per cent. The analysis reveals that the important discriminant expectation of SQFs among 'satisfies' and 'dissatisfies' are customer care and value added services which are higher among 'dissatisfies' than the 'satisfies'.

Perception on SQFS among The Customers of Various Service Providers

The customers are classified into customers are Airtel, Aircel, BSNL, Vodafone, Idea and Others. The level of perception on all service quality factor has been computed by the mean score of the perception on all service quality variables. The mean of perception on all SQFs among the customers of various service providers has been computed separately. The one way analysis of variance has been executed to analyse the significant difference among the six group of customers regarding the SERVPER scale on SQFs.

The Table 5.23 explains the mean, standard deviation and coefficient of variation of the perception score on all SQFs altogether. The highly perceived customers are the customers of Idea, Vodafone and Others, since their respective mean scores are 3.8225, 3.7173 and 3.6865. The higher consistency in perception is found among the customers of BSNL, since their respective coefficient of variation is 15.83 per cent. Regarding the SERVPERF scale on SQFs, the significant difference among the six group of customers has been found, since their respective 'F' statistics is significant at five per cent level.

Table 5.23: SERVPERF Scale on SQFs among the Customers of various Service Providers

Sl. No.	Service provider	Mean	Standard deviation	Coefficient of variation
1.	Airtel	3.6808	0.9189	24.96
2.	Aircel	3.2145	0.8602	26.76
3.	BSNL	3.0155	0.4773	15.83
4.	Vodafone	3.7173	0.8717	23.45
5.	Idea	3.8225	0.9096	23.79
6.	Others	3.6865	0.9245	25.07
	F-statistics 9.4508*			

*Significant at five per cent level.

Discriminant Service Quality among the Satisfies and Dissatisfies (Based on SERVPERF Scale)

The customers are classified into satisfies who have the overall attitude score of above 4, whereas, the customers who have the OAS of less than 2 is treated as dissatisfies. Out of 693 customers, there are 151 satisfies and 106 dissatisfies have been identified. It is imperative to identify the important SQFs among the satisfies and dissatisfies for some policy implications. The two group discriminant analysis have been executed to estimate the function. Initially, the mean difference, its 't' statistics and Wilks Lambda have been computed. These are presented in Table 5.24.

Table 5.24: Mean difference and discriminant power of SQFs satisfaction and dissatisfies (SERVPERF) scale

Sl.No.	SQFs	Mean score among		Mean Difference	't' statistics	Wilks Lambda
		Satisfies	Dissatisfies			
1.	Basic services (X_1)	3.9083	3.0451	-.8632	3.1408*	0.1408
2.	Value added services (X_2)	3.9089	3.1245	0.7844	3.0217*	0.1209
3.	Customer care (X_3)	3.9912	2.9341	1.0571	3.6869*	0.1311
4.	Responsiveness (X_4)	3.8644	3.2562	0.6082	2.3565*	0.2569
5.	Assurance (X_5)	3.7375	3.0814	0.6561	2.8144*	0.3445
6.	Recharge (X_6)	3.9082	2.9149	0.9933	3.2145*	0.4156

Regarding the perception (SERVPERF) on all SQFs, the significant mean difference among the satisfies and dissatisfies has been identified, since their respective 't' statistics are significant at five per cent level. The higher mean difference is identified in the case of customer care, recharge and basic services, since their respective mean differences are 1.0571, 0.9933, and 0.8632. The higher discriminant power is noticed in the case of value added services, customer care and basic services since their respective Wilks Lambda are 0.1209, 0.1311 and 0.1408.

The significant SQFs have been included for the establishment of Two group of discriminant function. The unstandardized procedure has been followed to estimate the function. The estimated function is:

$$Z = 1.2545 + 0.1447x_1 + 0.2809x_2 + 0.2911x_3 + 0.0865x_4 + 0.1013x_5 + 0.0962x_6$$

The relative contribution of discriminant SQFs in Total Discriminant score has been computed by the product of the discriminant coefficient and the mean difference of the respective SQFs. The results are given in Table 5.25.

Table 5.25: Relative contribution of discriminant SQFs in Total Discriminant Score (TDS)

Sl. No.	SQFs	Discriminant Coefficient	Mean Difference	Product	Relative contribution TDS
1.	Basic services	0.1447	0.8632	0.1249	14.39
2.	Value added services	0.2809	0.7844	0.2203	25.39
3.	Customer care	0.2911	1.0571	0.3077	35.47
4.	Responsiveness	0.0865	0.6082	0.0526	6.06
5.	Assurance	0.1013	0.6561	0.0665	7.66
6.	Recharge	0.0962	0.9933	0.0956	11.03
	Total			0.8676	100.00
	Per cent of cases correctly classified 74.07.				

The higher discriminant coefficient is noticed in customer care and value added service, since its coefficients are 0.2911 and 0.2809, respectively. It shows the higher degree of influence of the above-said two SQFs in discriminant function. The higher relative contribution in TDS is identified in the case of customer care and value added services, since its contributions are 35.47 and 25.39 per cent, respectively. The estimated discriminant function correctly classifies the case of satisfies and dissatisfies to the extent of 74.07 per cent. The analysis infers that the important discriminant SQFs among the satisfies and dissatisfies is the customers care and value added service, which are higher satisfiers compared to dissatisfies.

Discriminant Validity of the Service Quality Factors (SQFS)

The extent of mutually exclusiveness among the SQFs has been examined for further analysis. It is evaluated with the help of inter-correlation between the SQFs and their Average Variance Extracted by each Factor in service quality. If the Average Variance extracted by the SQF is greater than the sum of square of inter correlation between the Factor with other factors, the discriminant validity is confirmed. The inter-correlation coefficient between the SQFs are shown in Table 5.26.

Table 5.26: Inter correlation between SQFs (Based on Perception Score)

Sl. No.	Service quality factors (SQFs)	Basic service	Value added services	Customer care	Responsi-veness	Assurance	Recharge
1.	Basic services		0.1845	0.2642*	0.1717	0.1802*	0.2041*
2.	Value added services			0.2148*	0.2664*	0.1779*	0.2408*
3.	Customer care				0.2908*	0.2811*	0.1869*
4.	Responsiveness					0.1917*	0.1023
5.	Assurance						0.1449*
6.	Recharge						

*Significant at five per cent level.

The average variance extracted by Basic Services is 51.29 per cent, which is greater than the sum of square of inter correlation between the basic services with other services (20.75 per cent), which reveals the discriminant validity of basic services from other SQFs. Similarly, all other factors also prove their discriminant validity, since their respective Average Variance Extracted is greater than the sum of square of correlation between their SQF with other SQFs. Hence, the discriminant validity of SQFs has been confirmed.

Impact of Service Quality on the Overall Attitude towards their Services Provider in GSM Market

The present Study has made an attempt to analyse the impact of service quality factors in mobile phone service on the overall attitude towards the services in GSM Market in order to identify the important service quality factors. The perception score on six service quality factors has been included as the score of independent variables, whereas, the score on the overall attitude towards their service provider is taken as the score of dependent variable. The multiple regression analysis has been executed to analyse such impact. The fitted regression model is

$$Y = a + b_1x_1 + b_2x_2 + b_3x_3 + b_4x_4 + b_5x_5 + b_6x_6e$$

Whereas

Y = Score on overall attitude towards their service provider

X_1 = Score on the perception on basic service

X_2 = Score on the perception on value added services

X_3 = Score on the perception on customer care

X_4 = Score on the perception on responsiveness

X_5 = Score on the perception on assurance

X_6 = Score on the perception on recharge

$b_2, b_3 \ldots b_6$ = Regression co-efficient of independent variables

a = intercept and

e = error terms

The impact has been examined among the customers of Airtel, Aircel, Vodafone, BSNL, Idea and Virgin separately. The results are given in Table 5.27.

Table 5.27: Impact of perception on service quality on overall attitude towards GSM market

Sl. No.	Service quality	Regression co-efficients among customers in		
		Youngsters	Elders	Pooled
1.	Basic services	0.2903*	0.1721*	0.2144*
2.	Value added services	0.1141	0.0893	0.0911
3.	Customer care	0.2108*	0.1646*	0.1732*
4.	Responsiveness	0.2344*	0.2143*	0.2091*
5.	Assurance	0.1892*	0.2664*	0.2246*
6.	Recharge	0.1733*	0.1021	0.1193*
	Constant	1.1083	0.9334	1.0433
	R^2	0.7939	0.7217	0.8419
	F-statistics	10.3084*	9.3881*	13.1408*

*Significant at five per cent level.

From Table 5.27, it is inferred that the significantly influencing service quality factors on the overall attitude towards service provider among the young customers are basic of services, customer care, responsiveness, assurance and recharge. A unit increase in the perception on the above said factors results in an increase in the overall attitude towards their service providers by 0.2903, 0.2108, 0.2344m 0.1892 and 0.1733 units, respectively. The change in perception on service quality factors among young customers explains the changes in the overall attitude towards their service providers to the extent of 79.39 per cent. The significantly influencing service quality factors among the elders are basic services, customer care, responsiveness and assurance since the respective regression co-efficient are significant at five per cent level. The analysis of pooled data reveals that a unit increase in the perception on basic service, customer care responsiveness, assurance and recharge results in an increase in overall attitude towards the mobile phone service provider by 0.2144, 0.1732, 0.2091, 0.2246 and 0.1193 units respectively. The changes in the perception on service quality factors explain the changes in the overall attitude towards their service provider to the extent of 84.19 per cent. The significant 'F' statistics reveal the reliability of fitted regression model.

Impact of Service Quality on Overall Attitude towards Service Providers any Customers of Various Service Providers

The service providers in the mobile phone sector should know the significantly influencing service quality factors on their overall attitude towards the services. In the present study, an attempt has been made on analyzing the impact of service quality on overall attitude among the customers of various service providers. The multiple regression analysis has been administered to analyse such impact. The fitted regression model is

$$Y = a + b_1x_1 + b_2x_2 + b_3x_3 + b_4x_4 + b_5x_5 + b_6x_6e$$

Whereas

Y = Score on overall attitude towards their service provider
X_1 = Score on the perception on basic service
X_2 = Score on the perception on value added services
X_3 = Score on the perception on customer care
X_4 = Score on the perception on responsiveness
X_5 = Score on the perception on assurance
X_6 = Score on the perception on recharge
a = intercept and
e = error terms

The impact has been examined among the customers of Airtel, Aircel, Vodafone, BSNL, Idea and Virgin separately. The results are given in Table 5.28.

Table 5.28: Impact of Perception on Service Quality on Overall Attitude towards their Service Providers

Sl.No.	Service Quality	Regression Coefficient among Customers in					
		Airtel	Aircel	BSNL	Vodafone	Idea	Others
1.	Basic	0.2068*	0.1402*	0.2147*	0.1993*	0.2941*	0.1408*
2.	Value added services	0.433	0.0891	0.1113	0.1042	-0.0533	0.0614
3.	Customer care	0.0921	0.1911*	0.1304*	0.1987*	0.2082*	0.1236*
4.	Responsiveness	0.1868*	0.2033*	0.1729*	0.1453*	0.2147*	0.0737
5.	Assurance	0.1704*	0.1046	0.0962	0.1121	0.0733	0.0994
6.	Recharge	0.1001	0.1331*	0.1241*	0.1304*	0.2028*	0.2664*
	Constant	0.8943	0.6403	1.0344	0.9139	0.7183	1.0147
	R^2	0.7142	0.6511	0.9408	0.8234	0.5416	0.7616
	F-statistics	9.1109*	7.1084*	11.9308*	10.2646*	4.5861	10.3381*

*Significant at five per cent level.

Table 5.28 explains that among the Airtel customers, the significantly influencing service quality factors on the overall attitude towards the services offered are basic service, responsiveness and assurance, since its regression coefficients 0.2068, 0.1868 and 0.1704 are significant at five per cent level. The significantly influencing service quality factors among the customers of Airtel are basic service, customer care, responsiveness and recharge, whereas, among the customers of Vodafone, these factors are basic of service, customer care, responsiveness and recharge. Among the customers of BSNL, these factors are of basic services, customer care, responsiveness, and recharge and empathy. In the case of Idea, service quality factors have a significant impact on overall attitude towards their services provider which basic services, customer care, responsiveness and assurance, whereas, among the customers of others, these SQFs basic services, customer care and recharge.

REFERENCES

1. Holbrook, M.B. (1994), "The nature of customer value: an axiology of services in the consumption experience", in Rust, R-T and Oliver, R.C (Eds). Service Quality: New directions in Theory and practices, Sage publications, Inc. Thousand, Oaks, C.A., pp. 21-71.
2. Parasuraman, A., Zeithaml, V.A. and Berry, C.C. (1988), "SERVQUAL: A multiple–item scale for measuring consumer perceptions of service", *Journal of Retailing,* 64 (spring) pp. 12-40.
3. Garvin, D.A. (1988). *Management Quality: The Strategic and Competitive Edge,* The Free Press, New York,. NY.
4. Prahad, C.K. and Ramasamy, V. (2000), "Co-opting Customer Competencies", *Harvard Business Review,* January-February, pp.79-87.
5. Yonggui Wang and Hung-Polo (2002), "Service Quality, Customer satisfaction and behaviour intentions", *Journal of Service Marketing,* 41 (6), pp.50-60.
6. Leiser, Band Vance, C. (2001), "Cross-national assessment of service quality in the telecommunication industry: evidence from the USA and Germany", *Managing Service Quality,* 11(5), pp.307-317.
7. Peter, J.P. (1981), "Construct Validity: A Review of base Issues and Marketing Practices", *Journal of Marketing Research,* 18 (May), pp.133-145.
8. Yi (1990), "A critical review of consumer satisfaction", in Zeithmal, V.A., (Eds), *Review of Marketing 1990,* American Marketing Association, Chicago, IC, pp. 68-123.
9. Bettman, J.R., (1974), "A meshed model of attribute satisfaction decision", *Journal of Consumer Research,* Vol. I, September, pp. 30-35.
10. Swan, J.E and Oliver, R.C. (1985), "Automobile buyer satisfaction with the sales person related to equity and disconfirmation", in Hunk, H.K. and Day, R.C. (Eds) consumer satisfaction, Disconfirmation and complaining "Effects of expectations and disconfirmation on post exposure product Evaluation", *Journal of Applied Psychology,* 62(April), pp. 246-250.
11. Bearder, W.O. and Teel, J.E. (1983), "Selected Determinants of Consumer Satisfaction and Complaints Reports", *Journal of Marketing Research,* 20 (February), pp.21-28.

12. Oliver, R.C. (1981), "Measurement and Evaluation of Satisfaction Powers in Retail Settings", *Journal of Retailing,* 57 (Fall), pp.25-48.
13. Andreassen, T.W. (2000), "Antecedents to Satisfaction with Service Recovery", *European Journal of Marketing,* 34 (1&2), pp.156-175.
14. Oliver, R.C. (1993), "A conceptual Model of Service Quality and Service Satisfaction: Compatible Goals, different concepts", in Swantz, T.A., Bowen, D.E and Brown, SW (Eds). Advances in Marketing and Management, JAI Press, Inc., Green inch, Co-efficient, pp.65-85.
15. Anderson, EW and Sullivan, M.W (1993), "The antecedents and Consequences of customers Satisfaction for Firms", Marketing, 12 (Spring). pp.125-143.

6 Switching Behaviour and Customers Loyalty in the GSM Market

Introduction

The mobile phone service market is highly competitive. The expectations of customers from the service providers are also era changing. The customer reputation is a major task to the service provider because of the entrance of new comers into the market. Hence, it is essential to measure the future intention among the customers.

Distribution Based on Switching Behaviour

The switching behaviour among the customer is rated at five point scale, namely, definitely, positively, may be, no idea and never switching. The distribution of customers on the basis of their switching intention is illustrated in Table 6.1.

Table 6.1: Distribution of Customers on the Basis of their Switching Behaviour

Sl. No.	Switching Behaviour	Number of customers in		Total
		Youngsters	Elders	
1.	Definitely	214	84	298
2.	Positively	102	64	166
3.	May be	46	73	119
4.	No idea	28	31	59
5.	Never switch	23	28	51
	Total	**413**	**280**	**693**

Source: Primary data.

The important switching behaviour among the customers in definitely and positively switch over since it constitutes 43.00 and 23.95 per cent to the total, respectively. The customers are not willing to switch over constitute only 7.36 per cent to the total. The important switching behaviour among the youngsters are definitely and positively switch over, which constitutes 51.82 and 24.70 per cent to its total, respectively. Among the elder customers, these are definitely and positively switch over, since it constitutes 30.00 and 22.86 per cent to its total, respectively. The analysis reveals that the switching behaviour among the youngsters is greater than the elders.

Switching Behaviour among the Customers of Various Service Providers

The switching behaviour among the customers of various service providers has also been measured at five point scale in order to exhibit the level of switching behaviour among them. It is highly useful for the service provider to understand their customers behaviour. The distribution of customers of various service providers on the basis of their level of switching is given in Table 6.2.

Table 6.2: Switching behaviour in near Future

Sl. No.	Switching Behaviour	Number of Customers in GSM						Total
		Airtel	Aircel	Vodafone	BSNL	Idea	Others	
1.	Definitely	63	83	32	100	12	8	298
2.	Positively	32	51	19	44	8	12	166
3.	May be	14	21	20	43	7	14	119
4.	No idea	12	14	8	8	3	14	59
5.	Never switching	8	10	6	21	–	6	51
	Total	**129**	**179**	**85**	**216**	**30**	**54**	**693**

*Significant at five per cent level.

Table 6.2 reveals that the important switching intention among the customers of Airtel are definitely and positively since it constitutes 48.84 and 24.81 per cent to its total, respectively. Among the customers of Aircel, 28.49 per cent are positively switching over to other service providers, and 46.37 per cent are definitely switching over to other service providers. The important switching behaviour among the customers of Vodafone, the two are "definitely" and "may be" which constitute 37.65 and 23.53 per cent to its total, respectively. Among the customers of BSNL, these are definitely and positively switching over which constitute 46.29 and 20.37 per cent to its total, respectively. In the case of customers of Idea 40.00 per cent of the total customers definitely switch over to other service providers, whereas, among the customers of Others, it is only positively switch over which constitutes 22.22 per cent to its total. The analysis reveals that the higher switching intention is existing among the customers in GSM Market.

Variables Leading to Switching among the Customers

The switching intentions among the customers are influenced by various variables. The present Study confines these variables to network, free incoming, coverage, excellent service, tariff, security deposits, connectivity, attractive plans, Government cellular service, lesser switching cost, new operators brings less cost, new operators delivers expected service, better new recharge cost, innovative ideas, frequent offer, value added service, friends and relatives, popularity in the market, multi-usage, discount, free calls. Lesser subscription cost, extra benefits drawn from new operators, low premature termination of calls and comparative advantages. These variables are drawn from the reviews. The list of variables are shown in Table 6.3.

Table 6.3: Variables leading to Switching

Sl.No.	Variables
1.	Network
2.	Free incoming
3.	Coverage
4.	Excellent service
5.	Tariff
6.	Security deposits
7.	Connectivity
8.	Attractive plans
9.	Government cellular service
10.	Lesser switching cost
11.	New operator brings less cost
12.	New operator delivery expected service
13.	Better new recharge cost
14.	Innovative ideas
15.	Frequent offer
16.	Value added service
17.	Friends and relatives
18.	Popularity in the market
19.	Multi-usage
20.	Discount
21.	Free calls
22.	Lesser subscription cost
23.	Extra benefits drawn from new operators
24.	Low premature termination of calls
25.	Comparative advantage

From Table 6.3 it is inferred that the customers are asked to rate the above said twenty five variables at five point scale from highly important to not at all important. The assigned marks on these scales are from 5 to 1 respectively. The marks of the variables leading to switching among the customers are included for further analysis. The exploratory factor analysis is used to narrate the variables into important factors.

Factors Leading to Switching

The test of validity of data for factor analysis has been tested with the help of KMO measure of sampling adequacy and Bartlett's test of sphericity. The KMO measure of sampling adequacy is greater than the minimum acceptable level of 0.5. The chi-square value is also significant at zero per cent level. Since the above two tests satisfy the conditions for validity of data for factor analysis, the exploratory factor analysis has been administered. It results in five important factors. The variables in each factor, its eigen value and the per cent of variation explained are shown in Table 6.4.

Table 6.4: Factors leading to Switching

Sl. No.	Factors	Number of variables included	Eigen value	Per cent of variation explained	Reliability co-efficient
1.	Switching cost	8	4.8945	23.45	0.8402
2.	Service quality	6	4.1903	20.98	0.8189
3.	Pricing structure	5	3.0641	17.33	0.7063
4.	Network	3	2.2097	15.07	0.7241
5.	Environment	3	1.3408	12.11	0.6881
	Total	**25**		**88.94**	
	KMO measure of sampling adequacy: 0.8145			Bartlett's test of sphericity chi-square value: 81.09*	

*Significant at zero per cent level.

Table 6.4 explains that the narrated four factors explain the variables leading to switching to the extent of 88.94 per cent. The important factor leading to switching is switching cost, since its eigen value and per cent of variation explained are 4.8945 and 23.45 per cent, respectively. The second important factor is 'service quality', since its eigen value and the per cent of variation explained by it are 4.1903 and 20.98 per cent, respectively. The third important factor identified by the factor analysis is 'rate', since its eigen value and the per cent of variation explained are 3.0641 and 17.33 per cent, respectively. The last factors identified by the factor analysis are network and environment with the eigen value of 2.2097 and 1.3408, respectively. The per cent of variations explained by these factors are 15.07 and 12.11 per cent, respectively.

Reliability and validity of the Variables in 'Switching Cost'

In total, there are eight variables which have been included in the switching cost, since its factor loadings are higher in the switching cost compared to other Factors. In order to analyse the reliability and validity of variables in this Factor, the Confirmatory Factor Analysis (CFA) have been administered. The result of CFA is given in Table 6.5.

Table 6.5: Standardised Factor loading of the Variables in Switching Cost

Sl. No.	Variables	Standardised factor loading	t-statistics	Composite Reliability	Average Variance Extracted
1.	Lesser switching cost	0.9142	4.8145*	0.8145	59.62
2.	Comparative advantage	0.8645	4.0916*		
3.	Lesser subscription cost	0.8196	3.9334*		
4.	New operator brings less cost	0.7408	3.0818*		
5.	Extra benefits drawn from new operators	0.7311	2.9891*		
6.	New operators deliver expected service	0.7093	2.5616*		
7.	Low premature termination of calls	0.6865	2.3345*		
8.	Better new recharge cost	0.6217	2.1776*		
	Cronbach alpha 0.8402.				

*Significant at five per cent level.

The included eight variables in switching cost explain it to the extent of 84.02 per cent, since it's cronbach alpha is 0.8402. The 't' statistics of the standardized factor loading of the variables are significant at five per cent level. It reveals the convergent validity of the Factor. The standardized Factor loading is ranging from 0.9142 in lesser switching cost to 0.6217 in better new recharge cost. The convergent validity is also supported by the composite reliability and average variance extracted, since its values are greater than the minimum threshold of 0.5 and 50.00 per cent, respectively.

Reliability and Validity the variables in 'Service Quality'

The service quality Factor consists of six variables, namely, excellent service, value added service, innovative ideas, free calls, attractive plans and multi-usage, since its Factor loadings are higher in the service Factor than in other factors. The reliability and validity of the variables in 'service' Factor have been examined with the help of CFA. The standardized factor loading of the variables, its 't' statistics, composite reliability and average variance extracted by the Factor are illustrated in Table 6.6.

Table 6.6: Standardised Factor Loading of the Variables in Switching Cost

Sl. No.	Variables	Standardised factor loading	t-statistics	Composite Reliability	Average Variance Extracted
1.	Excellent service	0.9039	4.0145*	0.8021	55.44
2.	Value-added service	0.8204	3.4565*		
3.	Innovative ideas	0.7491	2.9146*		
4.	Free calls	0.6908	2.6081*		
5.	Attractive Plans	0.6144	2.5109*		
6.	Multi usage	0.5908	2.0118*		
	Cronbach alpha 0.8189.				

*Significant at five per cent level.

The 6.6 shows that the included six variables explain the service quality Factor to the extent of 81.89 per cent since its Cronbach Alpha is 0.8189. The higher standardized Factor loadings are noticed in the case of excellent service, value added service and innovative ideas, since its standardized Factor loadings are 0.9039, 0.8204 and 0.7491, respectively. The 't' statistics of the standardized Factor loadings of all variables are significant at five per cent level, which reveals the convergent validity. It is also supported by the composite reliability and average variance extracted, since these are greater than its standard minimum of 0.5 and 50.00 per cent, respectively. The analysis reveals that the included six variables are explaining the 'service quality' Factor to a reliable extent.

Reliability and validity of the Variables in 'Pricing Structure' Factor

The Variables, namely, discount, free incoming, tariff, security deposits and frequent offer are clustered into one Factor, since the Factor loadings are higher with pricing structure factor compared with other factors. The

Table 6.7: Standardised factor loading of the Variables in 'Pricing Structure Factor'

Sl. No.	Variables	Standardised factor loading	t-statistics	Composite Reliability	Average Variance Extracted
1.	Discount	0.8217	3.4511*	0.6844	52.45
2.	Free incoming	0.7203	2.7109*		
3.	Tariffs	0.6317	2.5241*		
4.	Security deposits	0.5943	2.0617*		
5.	Frequent offer	0.5720	1.9996*		
	Cronbach alpha 0.7063.				

*Significant at five per cent level.

standardized Factor loading of the variables, its 't' statistics, composite reliability, average variance explained and the reliability co-efficient are computed with the help of CFA in order to test the reliability and validity of variables in this Factor. The results are given in Table 6.7.

From Table 6.7, it is concluded that the reliability co-efficient of the factor is 0.7063. It infers that the included variables in 'pricing structure' Factor explain this Factor to the extent of 70.63 per cent. The standardized higher Factor loadings are noticed in the case of discount and free incoming, since the respective Factor loadings are 0.8217 and 0.7203. The 't' statistics of the standardized Factor loading of the variables are significant at five per cent level which reveals the convergent validity. It is also supported by the composite reliability and average variance extracted, since these two are greater than 0.5 and 50.00 per cent, respectively. The result reveals that the included variables in pricing structure factor to a reliable extent.

Reliability and Validity of the Variables in 'Network'

The 'Network' factor consists of three variables, namely, network, connectivity and coverage, since its Factor loadings are higher with the 'Network' factor compared to other Factors. The standardized Factor loadings of the variables, its 't' statistics, composite reliability, average variance extracted and the reliability co-efficient are computed to test the reliability and validity of variables in this Factor. The CFA has been executed for it. The result of CFA is presented in Table 6.8.

Table 6.8: Standardised factor loading of Variables in Network

Sl. No.	Variables	Standardised factor loading	t-statistics	Composite Reliability Co-efficient	Average Variance Extracted
1.	Network	0.8604	3.8081*	0.7049	51.23
2.	Connectivity	0.7241	0.5141*		
3.	Coverage	0.5844	2.1142*		
	Cronbach alpha 0.9241.				

*Significant at five per cent level.

Table 6.8 explains that the included three variables in 'Network' explain it to the extent of 72.41 per cent, since the respective reliability co-efficient is 0.7241. The 't' statistics of the standardized Factor loading of the variables in this Factor is significant at five per cent, which reveals the convergent validity. It is also supported by the composite reliability and average variance extracted, since these are greater than its minimum threshold of 0.50 and 50.00 per cent, respectively. The analysis indicates that the included three variables explain the network Factor to a reliable extent.

Reliability and Validity of the Variables in 'Environment'

The variables, namely, friends and relatives, popularity in the market and Government cellular service, are clustered into Environment Factor since its Factor loadings are higher in the Environment Factor than in other Factors. The reliability and validity of variables in 'Environment' Factor have been examined with the help of CFA. The standardized factor loading of the variables, 't' statistics, composite reliability, average variance extracted and reliability co-efficient of the factor are given in Table 6.9.

Table 6.9: Standardised factor loading of variables in environment

Sl. No.	Variables	Standardised factor loading	t-statistics	Composite Reliability Co-efficient	Average Variance Extracted
1.	Friends and Relatives	0.8743	3.4142*	0.6509	51.69
2.	Popularity in the market	0.6908	2.3081*		
3.	Government cellular service	0.5744	2.0042*		
	Cronbach alpha 0.6881.				

*Significant at five per cent level.

Table 6.9 reveals that the higher standardized factor loading is identified in friends and relatives' variable, since the respective Factor loading is 0.8743. The 't' statistics of the Factor loading of the variables are significant at five per cent level, which reveals the convergent validity. It is also supported by the composite reliability and average variance extracted, since these are 0.6509 and 51.69 per cent, respectively. The included three variables explain the factor to the extent of 68.81 per cent, since its cronbach alpha is 0.6881.

Customers Perception on Factor Leading to Switching in GSM Market

The customers in GSM Market analyse the merits and demerits of the existing systems and then to decide their switching behaviour. Hence, their Factor leading to switching from the existing service provider to other service provider may differ from customer to customer. The present Study has made an attempt to analyse the important Factors leading to switching among the young and older customers in GSM Market separately through the mean score of each Factor among them. In order to analyse the significant difference among the two groups of customers regarding their perception on the Factors leading to switching, the 't' test has been administered. The resultant mean score of the factors and their respective 't' statistics are illustrated in Table 6.10.

Table 6.10 shows that the highly perceived factors among the young customers in GSM Market are service quality and network, since the respective mean scores are 3.8471 and 3.7172, whereas, among the elder customers in GSM Market, these two are switching cost and price structure, since their mean scores are 3.8544 and 3.7339, respectively. Regarding the perception on the Factors leading to switching, the significant difference among the two groups of customers has been identified in the perception on all factors, since the respective 't' statistics are significant at five per cent level. The analysis reveals that important Factors leading to switching among youngsters is service quality and network, whereas, among elders, these are switching cost and price structure.

Table 6.10: Significant difference among the Young and Elder Customers in GSM Market

Sl. No.	Factors leading to switching	Mean score among the customers in		T-statistics
		Youngsters	Elders	
1.	Switching cost	2.9095	3.8544	–3.2176*
2.	Service quality	3.8471	3.0573	3.0244*
3.	Price structure	2.6068	3.7339	–3.8684*
4.	Network	3.7172	2.5648	3.4086*
5.	Environment	2.6061	3.4748	–2.8017*

*Significant at five per cent level.

Perception on the Factors Leading to Switching among the Customers of Various Service Providers

The customers are classified on the basis of their existing service providers. The mean scores on the perception on Factors leading to switching among the customers of different service providers is shown in order to exhibit the important Factors among them. The score of the Factors is drawn from the mean scores of the variables in each Factor. Regarding the perception on the factors, the significant difference among the seven groups of customers is analysed with the help of one-way analysis of variance.

Table 6.11: Significant difference among the Customers of various Service Providers

Sl. No.	Factors leading to switching	Mean Score among the Customers in						F-statistics
		Airtel	Aircel	BSNL	Vodafone	Idea	Others	
1.	Switching cost	3.4508	3.8144	2.8646	2.7145	3.0144	3.6169	2.8917*
2.	Service Quality	2.6083	3.1144	2.8904	2.5144	3.8941	3.3649	3.3146*
3.	Price structure	3.0173	3.8184	3.2344	2.9691	3.1718	2.5644	2.6508*
4.	Network	2.5417	2.9196	3.0649	2.4508	3.7081	3.0678	2.9193*
5.	Environment	2.3039	2.7671	2.7173	2.5681	3.6962	3.1142	2.2462*

*Significant at five per cent level.

Table 6.11 presents the mean scores of various Factors loading to switching and its respective 'F' statistics. The highly perceived Factor leading to switching among the customers of Airtel is printing cost and price structure, since the respective mean scores are 3.4508 and 3.0173. Among the customers of Airtel, these are price structure and switching cost, since their respective mean scores are 3.8184 and 3.8144.

Among the customers of Vodafone also, this is price structure and switching cost, since its mean scores are 2.9691 and 2.745, respectively. Among the customers of BSNL, these two are price structure and Network, since its mean scores are 3.2344 and 3.0649, respectively. The important Factor leading to switching among the customers of Idea are service Quality since its mean scores are 3.8941 and 3.7081, respectively. Among the customers of others, these two factors are switching cost and service quality, since its mean scores are 3.6169 and 3.3649, respectively. Regarding the perception on the Factors leading to switching, the significant differences among the customers of various service providers have been identified in the perception on all factors leading to switching, since the respective 'F' statistics are significant at five per cent level.

Association between the Profile of Customers and their Perception on Factors Leading to Switching

The profile of the customers may be associated with their perception on the Factors leading to switching. The included profile variables are sex, age, level of education, occupational ground, marital status, family size, personal income and family income. The one way analysis of variance has been executed to study the association between the profile of the customers and their perception on four factors leading to switching. The results are summarized in Table 6.12.

Table 6.12 explains that the significantly associating profile variables with the perception on the switching cost among the customers are then age, level of education, personal income, number of earning members per family and the personality score of the customers. Regarding the perception on 'service' Quality factor, the significantly associating profile variables are age, level of education, personal income number of earning member per family, family income and personality score, since the respective 'F' statistics are significant at five per cent level. The significantly associating profile variables in the perception on price structure are age, level of education, personal income number of earning members per family, family income, and personality score of the customers, whereas, in the perception on 'Network', these profile variables are occupational background, family size, personal income, number of members per family, family income and personality score. Regarding the perception on 'Environment' Factor, the significantly associating profile variables are level of education, occupational

Table 6.12: Association between Profile of Customer and their Perception on Factors leading to Switching

Sl.No.	Profile variables	F-statistics				
		Switching cost	Service	Price structure	Network	Environment
1.	Gender	3.0645	3.2408	2.9691	3.4508	3.6364
2.	Age	2.6865*	2.4517*	2.7086*	2.2101	1.9344
3.	Level of Education	2.8184*	2.5083*	2.4517*	1.9334	2.3089*
4.	Occupation background	1.3342	1.8914	2.0242	2.4039*	2.5244*
5.	Marital Status	1.0846	1.1409	2.1108	1.1732	2.3966*
6.	Family size	2.3011	2.1198	2.8906	2.4094*	2.6917*
7.	Personal Income	2.6811*	2.6047*	2.5133*	2.8183*	2.6133*
8.	Number of earning members per family	2.8188*	2.7667*	3.1414*	3.2168*	3.0844*
9.	Family Income	2.6182*	2.5154*	2.6027*	2.5659*	2.8024*
10.	Personality score	2.6566*	2.7082*	2.9192*	2.8184*	2.9697*

*Significant at five per cent level.

background, marital status, family size, personal income number of earning members in the family, family income, and personality score, since the respective 'F' statistics are significant at five per cent level.

Disriminant Switching Factors among the Young and Elder Customers

The importance given on the switching Factors among young and older customers may be different from each other. It is imperative to identify the important discriminant switching factors among the two group of customers in order to reduce the gap between the two group of customers and also to formulate appropriate marketing strategies to satisfy these two income groups. The two group discriminant analysis have been executed to identify the discriminant switching factors. Initially, the mean different, its 't' statistics and the wilks Lambda have been computed and presented in Table 6.13.

Table 6.13: Mean difference and Discriminant Power of the Factors among the Young and Elder Customers

Sl. No.	Switching factors	Mean score among the customers in		Mean Difference	t-statistics	Wilk's Lambda
		Youngsters	Elders			
1.	Switching cost (X_1)	2.9095	3.8544	-0.9449	-3.2176*	0.1899
2.	Service Quality (X_2)	3.8471	3.0573	0.7879	0.3.0244*	0.1341
3.	Price structure (X_3)	2.6068	3.7739	-1.1671	-3.8684*	0.1022
4.	Net work (X_4)	3.7172	2.5648	1.1524	3.4086*	0.3445
5.	Environment (X_5)	2.6061	3.4748	-0.8687*	-2.8017*	0.2861

*Significant at five per cent level.

The significantly mean difference among the youngster and eolder customers has been identified in all switching Factors source and their respective 't' statistics are significant at five per cent level. Its higher mean difference is identified in the case of price structure and Network, since their respective mean differences are -1.1671 and 1.1524. The higher discriminant power of switching Factors are identified in the case of price structure and service quality since their respective wilks Lambda co-efficients are 0.1022 and 0.1341. The significant switching factors have been included to estimate the two group discriminant function. The unstandardized procedure has been followed to estimate the function. The estimated function is:

$$Z = -\ 0.5455 - 0.1866x_1 + 0.385x_2 + -0.3217x_3 + 0.1014x_4 - 0.1718x_5$$

The relative contribution of the switching Factors in total discriminant Factor is computed by the product of the discriminant co-efficient and the mean difference of the respective switching Factor. The results are illustrated in Table 6.14.

Table 6.14: Relative Contribution of Factors in Total Discriminant Score

Sl. No.	Switching Factors	Discriminant Co-efficients	Mean Difference	Product	Relative Contribution in TDS
1.	Switching cost	-0.1866	-0.9449	.1763	16.61
2.	Service Quality	0.3085	0.7879	0.2436	22.95
3.	Price structure	-0.3217	-1.1671	.3755	35.37
4.	Network	0.1014	1.1524	0.1168	11.01
5.	Environment	-0.1718	-0.8687	.1492	14.06
	Total			**1.0614**	**100.00**
Per cent of cases correctly classified : 79.08					

The higher discriminant co-efficient is identified in the case of price structure and service quality, since their respective mean differences are -0.3217 and 0.3085. It infers that the above said two switching factors have more influence in the discriminant function. The higher relative contribution of switching factors in TDS is noticed in the case of price structure and service quality, since its relative contributions are 35.37 and 22.95 per cent, respectively. The per cent of cases correctly classified by the function is 79.08. The analysis reveals that the important discriminant switching factors among the young and elder customers are price structure and service quality.

Discriminant Validity among the Switching Factors

The discriminant validity among the switching Factors has been computed with the help of Average Variance Extracted (AVE) by the Factor and their inter-correlation, co-efficient among various factors. If the AVE of the switching Factor is greater than the sum of square of inter correlation between the Factor with the other factors, its discriminant validity has been confirmed. The computed inter correlation between the various switching factors is given Table 6.15

Table 6.15: Inter Correlation between the Switching Factors

Sl. No.	Switching Factors	Switching Cost	Service Quality	Price structure	Network	Environ-ment
1.	Switching cost		0.1344	0.2817*	0.1089	-0.1403
2.	Service Quality			-0.1891*	0.2025*	0.1089
3.	Price statement				-0.1814*	0.2142*
4.	Network					0.1884*
5.	Environment					

*Significant at five per cent level.

The significant correlation is identified between source of the switching Factors. The Average Variance Extracted by switching cost (59.62 per cent) is greater than the sum of square of inter correlation co-efficients between switching cost and other factors (12.89%). Hence, its discriminant validity is confirmed. Similarly in the case of service of quality, AVE is 55.44 per cent, whereas, the sum of square of correlation co-efficient between service quality and other factor is only 10.67 per cent. In all other switching Factors, its respective AVE is greater than the sum of square correlation co-efficient between the respective Factor with other Factors. It reveals the discriminant validity among the switching Factors.

Impact of Switching Factors on the Switching Behaviour among the Customer

The identified switching Factors in the GSM Market among the customers are switching cost, service quality, price structure, Net work and environment. It is important to analyse the relative importance of each switching factor on the switching intention among the customer for some policy implications. The multiple regression analysis has been executed to analyse the impact. The Ordinary Least Square (OLS) has been executed to fit the function. The fitted regression model is:

$$Y = a + b_1x_1 + b_2x_2 + b_3x_3 + b_4x_4 + b_5x_5 + e$$

Whereas

Y = Score on Switching intention among the customers

X_1 = Score on switching cost intention among the customers

X_2 = Score on service quality among the customers

X_3 = Score on price structure among the customers

X_4 = Score on Network among the customers

X_5 = Score on Environment among the customers

$b_1, b_2, \ldots b_5$ = regression co-efficient of independent variables

a = intercept and

e = error term

The impacts of switching factor have been examined among the young, old and also for pooled data. The results are given in Table 6.16.

Table 6.16: Impact of Switching Factors on Switching Intention

Sl. No.	Factors	Regression co-efficient among customers in		
		Youngsters	Elders	Pooled Data
1.	Switching cost	0.1082	0.2403*	0.1596*
2.	Service Quality	0.2873*	0.0842	0.2011*
3.	Price structure	0.1144	0.2776*	0.2403*
4.	Net work	0.2304*	0.2331*	0.2245*
5.	Environment	-0.0886	0.1509*	0.0911
6.	Constant	0.8431	1.3085	0.9909
7.	R^2	0.7336	0.7042	0.8454
8.	F-statistics	8.9081*	7.9909*	11.3345*

*Significant at five per cent level.

The significantly and positively influencing switching factors on the switching behaviour among the youngsters have been identified in the case of service quality and network, since their respective regression co-efficients are significant at five per cent level. A unit increase in the above-said switching factors result in an increase in switching intention among the young customers by 0.2873 and 0.2304 unit, respectively.

Among the older customers, these switching Factors are switching cost, price structure, net work and environment, since their respective regression co-efficients are significant at five per cent level. A unit increase in the above-said switching factors result in an increase in switching intention by 0.2403, 0.2776, 0.2331 and 0.1509 units, respectively. The charge in the importance given on switching factors explain the charges in the switching to intention among the elder customers is 70.42 per cent, since its R^2 is 0.7042. The analysis of pooled data reveals the importance of switching cost, service quality, price structure and net-work on the switching intention among the customers in total. The charges in the importance given on the switching factors explain the charges in switching intention among the customers to the extent of 84.54 per cent, since its R^2 is 0.8454.

Impact of Switching Factors on Switching Intention among the Customers of Various Service Providers

The impact of switching factors on the switching intention among the customers of Airtel, Aircel, BSNL, Vodafone, Idea and Others has been computed separately with the help of multiple regression analysis. The result of multiple analysis is shown in Table 6.17.

Table 6.17: Impact of Switching Factors on Switching Intention

Sl. No.	Switching Factors	Regression co-efficient among customers in					
		Airtel	Aircel	BSNL	Vodafone	Idea	Others
1.	Switching cost	0.1901*	0.2413*	0.1417*	0.2411*	0.1456*	0.2089*
2.	Service quality	0.1052	0.1565*	0.0899	0.1885*	0.1668*	0.1884*
3.	Price structure	0.2402*	0.0461	0.2462*	0.2084*	0.1081	0.1609*
4.	Network	0.0561	0.2108*	-0.0893	0.1903*	0.1246	0.2433*
5.	Environment	-0.0992	0.0544	0.1017	0.0961	0.0993	0.1139
6.	Construct	0.7345	0.9891	0.6544	0.9145	0.5045	0.9849
	R^2	0.7962	0.7609	0.8109	0.7508	0.6867	0.6917
	F-statistics	9.4508*	8.1401*	10.1454*	8.0236*	7.4509*	7.9964*

*Significant at five per cent level.

Regarding the customers of Airtel, the significantly influencing switching Factors on the switching intention are switching cost and price structure, since their respective regression co-efficients are 0.1901 and 0.2402. A unit increase in the above said two switching factors result in an increase in switching intention by 0.1901 and 0.2402 units, respectively. Among the customers of Aircel, a unit increase in the switching cost, service quality and network result in an increase in the switching intention by 0.2413, 0.1565 and 0.2108 units, respectively. The changes in the importance given on switching Factors explain the charges in the switching intention of the customers of Airtel to the extent of 76.09 per cent since its R^2 is 0.7609.

The significantly influencing switching factors on the switching intention among the customers of BSNL is switching cost and price structure, since their respective regression co-efficients are significant at five per cent level. Change in the importance given on switching Factors explain the changes in switching intention among the customers of BSNL to the extent of 81.09 per cent. Among the customers of Vodafone, a unit increase in the importance given on switching cost, service quality, price structure and network result in an increase in switching intention by 0.2411, 0.1885, 0.2084 and 0.1903 units, respectively.

Among the customers of Idea, the significantly influencing switching factors on the switching intentions are switching cost and service quality, whereas, among the customers of Others, these factors are switching cost, service quality, price structure and network. The change in the importance given on switching factors explain the changes in switching intention among the customers of Idea and Others to the extent of 68.67 and 69.17 per cent level, respectively.

Overall Attitude Towards Service Provider and Switching Behaviour among the Customers

The switching behaviour among the customers has been measured at five point scale, namely, definitely, positively, may be, no idea, and never switching. Similarly, the overall attitude score (OAS) has been confined to less than 2.0, 2.0 to 3.00; 3.01 to 4.00 and above 4.00. It is imperative to analyse whether less the satisfied customers are willing to switch over from the existing service provider or all customers are willing to switch over irrespective of their OAS. Hence, the present Study has made an attempt to identify the number of customers with different level of OAS and degree of switching intentions. The results are given on Table 6.18.

Table 6.18: Over all Attitude (OAS) towards Existing Service Provider and the Switching behaviour among Customers

Sl. No.	Switching Intentions	OAS				Total
		Less than 2.0	2.0-3.0	3.0-4.00	Above 4.00	
1.	Definitely	43	64	146	45	298
2.	Positively	21	37	66	42	166
3.	May be	29	27	42	21	119
4.	No Idea	13	22	20	4	59
5.	Never switching	-	3	9	39	51
	Total	**106**	**153**	**283**	**151**	**693**

Source: Primary data.

It is interesting to note that the satisfied and highly satisfied customers are also willing to switch over to other service providers, since they constitute 64.09 per cent to the total number of customers who mentioned definitely switch over. The number of customers who are willing to switch on constitutes only 7.36 per cent to the total of 693 customers. Out of 166 customers mentioning "positively switch over to other service providers", 65.05 per cent are having an OAS of 3.00. The analysis reveals that the OAS among the customers is not the criteria for their switching intention. Even the highly satisfied customers are willing to switch on because of some reasons.

Discriminant Switching Factors among the Satisfied and Dissatisfied Customers

The customers are classified into "satisfiers" and "dissatisfies" on the basis of their OAS already. In total, there are 151 satisfies and 106 dissatisfies. It is imperative to identify the important discriminant switching factors among the two groups for some policy implication. The score on five switching factors among the two groups of customers has been included for two group discriminant analysis. Initially, the mean difference, its 't' statistics and the Wilk's Lambda of the switching factors are computed and presented in Table 6.19.

Table 6.19: Mean difference and Discriminant Power of the Switching Factors among the Satisfies and Dissatisfies

Sl. No.	Switching Factors	Mean score among the customers in		Mean Difference	t-statistics	Wilk's Lambda
		Satisfies	Dissatisfies			
1.	Switching cost (X_1)	2.8568	3.7024	-0.8456	-3.0514*	0.1408
2.	Service Quality (X_2)	3.1745	3.8144	-0.0999	-0.3149	0.1865
3.	Price (X_3)	2.4586	3.6046	-1.1460	-3.4082*	0.1317
4.	Net work (X_4)	2.6568	3.7165	-1.0597	-3.1776*	0.2865
5.	Environment (X_5)	2.9969	3.45623	-0.4593	-1.4085	0.3785

*Significant at five per cent level.

The higher mean difference among the "satisfiers" and "dissatisfiers" have been identified in the case of price structure and network, since their respective mean differences are –1.1460 and –1.0597. The significant mean differences are identified in the case of switching cost, price structure and network, since their respective 't' statistics are significant at five per cent level. The higher discriminant power is identified in the case of price structure and switching cost their respective Wilk's Lambda co-efficients are 0.1317 and 0.1408. The significant switching factors have been included for the establishment of two group discriminant function. The unstandardized procedures have been followed to estimate the function. The estimated function is

$$Z = -1.2341 - 0.3242x_1 - 0.3085x_3 - 0.2961x_4$$

The relative contribution of discriminant switching factors in Total Discriminant score is computed by the product of the discriminant co-efficient and the mean difference of the respective factors. The results are presented in Table 6.20.

Table 6.20: Relative Contribution of Discriminant Factors in Total Discriminant Score (TDS)

Sl. No.	Factors	Discriminant co-efficient	Mean Difference	Product	Relative contribution in TDS
1.	Switching cost	-0.3246	-0.8456	0.2745	29.15
2.	Price structure	-0.3085	-1.1460	0.3535	37.53
3.	Network	-0.2961	-1.0597	0.3138	33.32
	Total			**0.9418**	**100.00**
Per cent of cases correctly classified: 71.07					

The higher discriminant co-efficient is identified in the case of switching cost and price structure, since their respective co-efficients are -0.3246 and -0.3085. It shows the higher influence of the above-said two factors in the discriminant function. The higher contribution in TDS is noticed in the case of price structure and network, since their relative contribution, are 37.53. The estimated discriminant function correctly classifies the cases to the extent of 71.07 per cent. The analysis indicates the cases to the extent of 71.07 per cent. The analysis indicates that the important discriminant switching factors among the "satisfies" and "dissatisfies" are the price structure and network, which are relatively high among the 'dissatisfiers' than the 'satisfiers'.

Customers Loyalty in the Mobile Telecommunication Market

The continuous success of a Firm rests on its capability to retain its current customers and make them loyal of its brands (Dekimpe *et al.*, 1997)[1]. Loyal customers build businesses by buying more, paying premium prices, and providing new referrals through positive word of mouth over time (Ganesh et al., 2000)[2]. In fact, companies in telecommunication are losing 2 to 4 per cent of their customers monthly; disloyal customers can amount to millions of lost revenue and profit (Serkan and Gokhan, 2005)[3]. The two basic approaches to study customer loyalty, (Oliver, 1999)[4] namely, stochastic and deterministic loyalty.

The stochastic approach assumes customers loyalty as a behavuiour (Ehrenberg, 1988)[5]. The used operational measures are shares of purchase, purchasing frequency, etc. In the deterministic approach, customer loyalty is an attitude (Fournier and Yao, 1977)[6]. The used operational measures are preference, buying intention, supplier prioritization and recommendation willingness. In the present Study, the deterministic approach has been followed to measure the customer loyalty.

The behavioural measures of customer loyalty was operatinalized by Farley, 1964[7] ; Brown, 1952[8]; Boulding et al., 1993 [9]; Narayandas, 1996[10]; Kim et al., 2004[11]; Gerpost et al., 2001[12]; Lee and Cunninghan, 2001[13];

Table 6.21: Variables in Customer Loyalty

Sl.No.	Variables
1.	Continue with current service provider
2.	Wish to have one more connection
3.	Pride of my service provider
4.	Recommend my service provider to others
5.	Higher trust on my service provider
6.	Inclination to buy other services
7.	Lesser price sensitive
8.	Service differentiation from my service provider
9.	Competitive advantage my service provider
10.	No other alternative to my service provider.

Chadha and Kappor, 2009[14]; and Ashish Dash, 2007)[15]. The variables related to the measurement of the customer loyalty in the mobile telecommunication market have been derived from the above reviews. These are listed in Table 6.21.

The customers are asked to rate the above-said ten variables at five point scale according to their attitude from highly agree to highly disagree. The assigned scores on these scales are from 5 to 1, respectively.

Customers' Perception on Variables in Customer Loyalty

The score of the variables related to customer loyalty among the young and older customers have been computed to exhibit their level of loyalty towards their service providers. The 't' test has been administered to find out the significant difference among the young and older customers regarding their perception on the variables related to customer loyalty. The results are shown in Table 6.22.

Table 6.22: Customers' Perception on variables in Customer Loyalty towards their Service Provider

Sl.No.	Variables	Mean score among customers in		t-statistics
		Youngsters	Elders	
1.	Continue the present service provider	2.0456	2.7347	-3.1442*
2.	Wish to have one more connection	1.3414	1.6408	-0.9086
3.	Pride of my service provider	1.8909	2.8245	-3.0149*
4.	Recommend my service provider to others	2.2452	2.6561	-0.9983
5.	Higher trust on my service provider	1.6644	2.5084	-3.0843*
6.	Inclination to buy other services	1.8843	2.3341	-1.8083
7.	Lesser price sensitive	1.3408	2.4144	-2.3969*
8.	Service differentiation from my service provider	2.5086	2.9092	-1.5616
9.	Competitive advantage from my service provider	2.4144	2.7368	-0.9085
10.	No other alternative to my service provider	1.4664	2.5616	-2.8644*

*Significant at five per cent level.

The highly perceived variables among the young customers is service differentiation from my service provider and competitive advantage from my service provider, since their respective mean scores are 2.5086 and 2.4144. Among the older customers, these two are service differentiation from my service provider and pride of my service provider, since their respective mean scores are 2.9092 and 2.8245. Among the young and older customers, the significant difference has been noticed in the perception on continue the present service provider, pride of my service provider, higher trust on my service provider, since their respective 't' statistics are significant at five per cent level.

Reliability and Validity of Variables in Customer Loyalty

In total, 10 variables have been included for measurement of customer loyalty. The score of the 10 variables among the customers has been included to test its reliability and validity with the help of Confirmatory Factor Analysis (CFA). The standardized factor loading of the variables, its 't' statistics, composite reliability, average variance extracted and the reliability co-efficient of the construct have been computed and presented in Table 6.23.

Table 6.23: Standardized Factor loadings of the Variables in Customer Loyalty

Sl. No.	Variables	Standardized factor loading	't' statistics	Composite reliability	Average Variance Extracted
1.	Competitive advantage from my service provider	0.9262	4.2456*	0.7941	54.03
2.	Recommend my service provider to others	0.8504	3.8149*		
3.	Pride of my service provider	0.8149	3.6108*		
4.	Continue the present service provider	0.7906	3.4514*		
5.	Lesser price sensitive	0.7517	3.0996*		
6.	Wish to have one more connection	0.7082	2.8234*		
7.	Service differentiation from my service provider	0.6911	2.7149*		
8.	Higher trust on my service provider	0.6502	2.3446*		
9.	Inclination to buy other services	0.6099	2.1408*		
10.	No other alternative to my service provider	0.5845	2.0044*		
Cronbach alpha 0.8149.					

The 't' statistics of the standardized factor loading of the variables are significant at five per cent level, which reveals the convergent validity of the construct. It is also supported by the composite reliability and average variance extracted, since these are greater than its standard minimum of 0.5 and 50.00 per cent respectively. The included 10 variables in the customer loyalty explain it to the extent of 81.49 per cent, since its cronbach alpha is 0.8149. The analysis infers that the included 10 variables in the construct explain to a reliable extent.

Customer Loyalty Score (CLS) among the Customers

The Customer Loyalty Score (CLS) among the customers has been measured with the help of the mean score of the variables related to customer loyalty.

The CLS in the present Study is confined to less than, 2.0; 2.00 to 3.00; 3.01 to 4.00 and above 4.00. The distribution of customers on the basis of their CLS is given in Table 6.24.

Table 6.24: Customer Loyalty Score (CLS) among the Customers

Sl.No.	CLS	Number of customers in		Total
		Youngsters	Elders	
1.	Less than 2.0	274	141	415
2.	2.0-3.00	93	86	179
3.	3.01-4.00	46	39	85
4.	Above 4.0	-	14	14
	Total	**413**	**280**	**693**

Source: Primary data

The important CLS among the customers in the Study area is less than 2.00 and 2.00 to 3.00, which constitutes 59.08 and 25.83 per cent to the total, respectively. The customers with the CLS of above 4.00 constitutes 2.02 per cent to the total. The most important CLS among the young customers is less than 2.00, which constitutes 66.34 per cent to its total. Among the older customers, this is also less than 2.0, which constitutes 50.36 per cent to its total. Thc analysis reveals that the loyalty is very poor among the customers. It is extremely poor among the young customers than the older customers.

Customer Loyalty Score among the Customers of various Service Providers

The Customer Loyalty Score (CLS) among the customers of various service quality has been measured to exhibit the level of customer loyalty towards various service providers in the market. The mean, standard deviation and co-efficient of variation of CLS have been computed among the customers of different service providers. The one way analysis of variance has been applied to analyse the significant difference among the different group of customers regarding their CLS. The results are given in Table 6.25.

Table 6.25: Customer Loyalty score (CLS) among the Customers of various Service Providers

Sl. No.	Service provider	Mean	Standard deviation	Co-efficient of variation
1.	Airtel	2.0317	0.3441	16.94
2.	Air cel	2.0541	0.4802	23.38
3.	BSNL	2.3688	0.2614	11.03
4.	Vodafone	2.0144	0.3302	16.39
5.	Idea	2.0842	0.4314	20.69
6.	Others	2.0431	0.4092	20.03
		F-statistics : 1.7984		

The higher Customer Loyalty Score is seen among the customers in BSNL, but the mean score is only 2.3688. The higher consistency in the customer loyalty is also seen among the customers of BSNL, since their respective co-efficient of variation is 11.03 per cent. The one way analysis of variance infers that there is no significant difference among the customers of different service providers regarding their customer loyalty since their respective F-statistics is not significant at five per cent level.

Association between the Profile of Customers and their CLS

Since the profile of the customers may be associated with their level of customer loyalty towards their service provider, the present Study has made an attempt to analyse this aspect with the help of one way analysis of variance. The included profile variables are gender, age, level of education, occupational, background, marital status, family size, personal income, number of earning members per family, family income and personality score. The result of one way analysis of variance is given in Table 6.26.

Table 6.26: Association between Profile of Customers and then CLS

Sl. No.	Profile Variables	F-statistics	Table Value of 'F' at five per cent level	Result
1.	Gender	3.0452	3.84	Insignificant
2.	Age	3.1441	2.37	Significant
3.	Level of Education	2.4544	2.21	Significant
4.	Occupational background	2.0899	2.21	Insignificant
5.	Marital status	2.1144	2.37	Insignificant
6.	Family size	2.0815	2.37	Insignificant
7.	Personal income	2.5614	2.37	Significant
8.	Number of earning members per family	2.6114	2.60	Significant
9.	Family income	2.6545	2.37	Significant
10.	Personality score	3.1485	2.60	Significant

The significantly associating profile variables with the CLS of the customers are their age, level of education, personal income, number of earning members per family, family income and personality score, since their respective 'F' statistics are significant at five per cent level. The results indicate that there is an association between the profile of the customers and their customer loyalty score on their service providers.

Overall Attitude and Customer Loyalty Towards their Service Providers

The level of satisfaction towards the service provider of the customers has been measured by Overall Attitude Score (OAS). The customer loyalty has been measured by Customer Loyalty Score (CLS). All satisfied customer may be loyal or not loyal to their service provider. The overall attitude is one of the essential factors lead to the customer loyalty. Hence the present Study has made an attempt to analyse this aspect with the help of OAS and CLS among the customers. The distraction of customers on the basis of their OAS and CLS is illustrated in Table 6.27

Table 6.27: Overall Attitude and Customer Loyalty among the Customers

Sl. No.	OAS/CLS	Less than 2.00	2.00–3.00	3.01–4.00	Above 4.00	Total
1.	Less than 2.0	88	119	119	89	415
2.	2.0-3.0	18	17	107	37	179
3.	3.01-4.00	-	12	52	21	85
4.	Above 4.00	-	5	5	4	14
	Total	**106**	**153**	**283**	**151**	**693**

Source: Primary data.

The highly satisfied customers who are with the OAS of above 3.00 may be disloyal to their service provider. It is seen in an analysis where it is mentioned that 77.53 per cent of the customers with the OAS of above 3.00 are having a CLS of less than 3.01. The number of customers with the high OAS of above 4 and high CLS of above 4.00 constitutes only 2.65 per cent to its total. The analysis infers that the OAS will not provide any guarantee of customer loyalty to their service provider.

Impact of Switching Factors on Customer Loyalty

The importance given on switching factors may have its own impact on the customer loyalty. In order to analyse the impact, the multiple regression analysis has been executed. The fitted regression model is:

$$Y = a + b_1x_1 + b_2x_2 + b_3x_3 + b_4x_4 + b_5x_5 + e$$

Whereas Y = Customer loyalty score among the customers

X_1 = Score on switching cost among the customers

X_2 = Score on service Quality among the customers

X_3 = Score on price structure among the customers

X_4 = Score on Net work among the customers

X_5 = Score on environment among the customers

$b_1, b_2, \ldots b_5$ = regression co-efficient of independent variables

a = intercept

e = error term

The impact analysis has been done among the youngsters, elders and also for pooled data. The results are given on Table 6.28.

The significantly switching factors on the customer loyalty among the young customers are switching cost and price structure. A unit increase in above-said two factors result in a decline in customer loyalty by 0.2844 and 0.2149 units, respectively. The charges in the importance given on switching factors explain the charges in the customer loyalty to the extent of 81.49 per cent, since its R^2 is .8149. Among the older customers, the significantly influencing switching factors are the same, but their regression co-efficients are -0.2133 and -0.3245. The charges in the importance given on switching factors explain the charges in CLS among the older customers to the extent of 68.41 per cent.

Table 6.28: Impact of Switching Factors on Customer Loyalty

Sl. No.	Switching Factors	Regression co-efficient among customers in		
		Youngsters	Elders	Pooled
1.	Switching cost	-0.2833*	-0.2133*	-0.2482*
2.	Service Quality	0.1025	0.1133	0.1011
3.	Price structure	-0.2149*	-0.3245*	-0.2738*
4.	Network	-0.1011	0.0891	-0.0445
5.	Environment	0.1233	0.1143	0.1039
	Construct	-0.9439	-0.6841	-0.8349
	R^2	0.8149	0.7249	0.8841
	F-statistics	10.4938*	7.8546*	12.4938*

*Significant at five per cent level.

Impact of Switching Factors on Customer Loyalty among the Customers of Various Service Providers

The impact of switching factors on CLS among the customers of Airtel, Aircel, BSNL, Vodafone, Idea and Others has been examined separately with the help of multiple regression analysis. The results are presented in Table 6.29.

Table 6.29: Impact of Switching Factors on Customer Loyalty among Customers of various Service Providers

Sl. No.	Switching Factors	Regression co-efficient among customers in					
		Airtel	Aircel	BSNL	Vodafone	Idea	Others
1.	Switching cost	-0.1898*	-0.2149*	-0.2864*	-0.2344*	-0.1908*	-0.2144*
2.	Service Quality	-0.1449*	0.0914	0.0441	-0.1908*	-0.0933	0.0917
3.	Price structure	-0.1884*	-0.1802*	-0.1917*	-0.1433*	0.0344	-0.1346*
4.	Net work	-0.0916	-0.1564*	0.0245	-0.1661*	-0.1817*	0.0344
5.	Environment	0.1024	0.0896	0.1122	0.0844	-0.1922*	-0.1345*
6.	Construct	-0.6817	-0.8142	-0.6861	-0.7137	-0.5633	-0.7644
	R^2	0.7314	0.7549	0.8142	0.7029	0.6844	0.7149
	F-statistics	8.1402*	8.6818*	10.1718*	7.8444*	7.0143*	7.6086*

*Significant at five per cent level.

Among the customers of Airtel, the significantly influencing switching factors on CLS are switching cost, service quality and price structure. A unit increase in the importance given on above-said factors result in a decline in CLS by 0.1898, 0.1449 and 0.1884 units, respectively. The changes in the importance given on switching factors explain the charges in CLS by 73.14 per cent, since their R^2 is 0.7314. Among the customers of Aircel, these switching factors are switching cost, price structure and Net work, since their respective regression co-efficients are -0.2149, -0.1802 and -0.1564. The changes in the importance given on switching factors explain the charges in CLS among the customer of Airtel to the extent of 75.49 per cent.

The significantly influencing switching factors among the customers of BSNL are switching cost and price structure, since their respective regression co-efficients are significant at five per cent level. The co-efficient of determination (R^2) is 0.8142. Among the customers of Vodafone, the significantly influencing switching factors are switching cost service quality, price structure and network. A unit increase in the above-said factors result in a decline by 0.2344, .0.1908, 0.1433 and 0.1661 units, respectively. Among the customers of Idea, a unit increase in the importance given on switching cost, network and environment result in a decline in CLS by 0.1908, 0.1817 and 0.1922 units, respectively. Among the customers of Others, the significantly and negatively influencing switching factors are switching cost, price structure and environment. The co-efficient of determination is 0.7149. It reveals that the changes in the perception on switching factors explain the changes in customers loyalty to the extent of 71.49 per cent.

Linkage Between Service Quality Factors, Overall Attitude and Customer Loyalty

Numerous influencing factors have lead to corporation-boundaries losing their character and alternative forms of organization (Child and Faulkner, 1998)[16]. The intangible factors, such as, knowledge, customer relation, innovation, etc. play a major role in the Corporations' success (Gulati, 1998)[17]. A basic assumption of this analysis is that measurement like basic services, value added services, customer care, responsiveness, assurance and recharge, which eventually lead to the organizational performance (both overall attitude and customer loyalty). Regarding the factors influencing the customer loyalty, many studies focus on the customers' satisfaction as the determinations. But the present Study has made an attempt to incorporate the service quality as the determinations of customer loyalty. (Serkan and Ozer, 2004)[18]. The direct and in direct effect of determinants on the customer loyalty have been measured with the help of Structural Equation Modelling (SEM) as did by Klaus (2009)[19] The path diagram is shown in below.

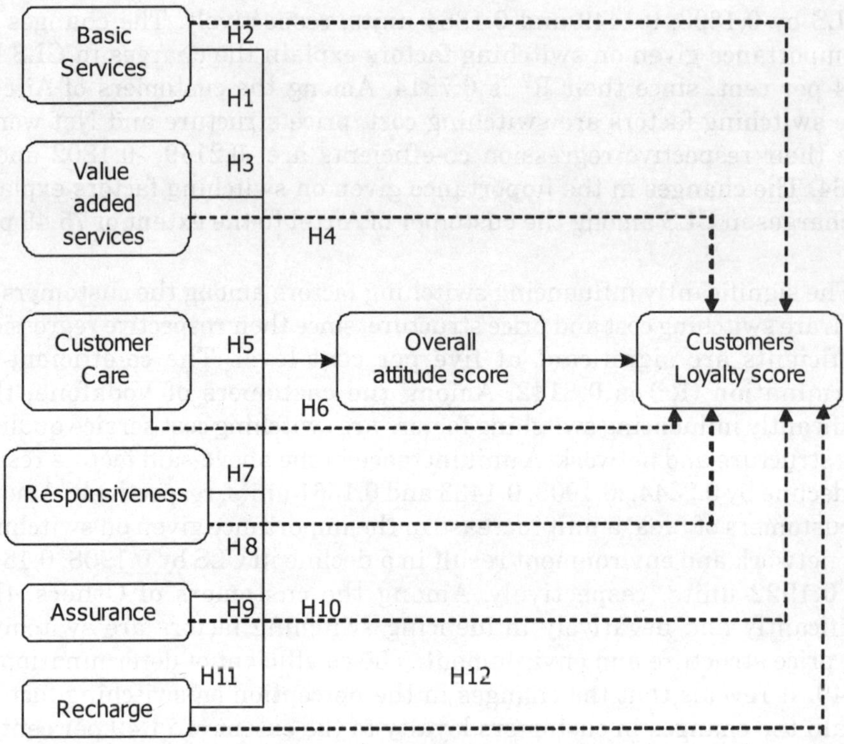

Fig. 6.1. Path Diagram

The above-said path diagram indicates both direct and in direct effect of influencing factors on the out come variable (Customer Loyalty). The hypotheses, namely, H_1, H_3, H_5,H_7,H_9, $H_{11}$and H_{13} are showing the direct effect of influencing factors on customer loyalty. The hypothesis, namely, H_2, H_4, H_6, H_8, H_{10} and H_{12} are indicating the effect of influencing factors on customer loyalty through the moderate variable, namely, overall attitude towards service provider.

Goodness of Fit Statistics

The proposed model was tested with AMOS 5.0 version. On the whole, the goodness of fit indices resulted in a satisfying model fit. The indices namely chi-square, standardized root mean square residual, comparative fit index (CFI) Adjusted Goodness-Fix Index (AGFI) and Normed Fit Index (NFI) have been computed and presented in Table 6.30.

The chi-square statistics (x^2), standardized Root Mean Square Residual (RMR), Goodness of Fit Index (GFI), Adjusted Goodness-of-Fit Index (AGFI), Comparative Fit Index (CFI) and Normed Fit Index (NFI) indicate that the

Table 6.30: Fit Indices of the Research Model

Sl. No.	Items	Co-efficient
1.	Chi-square	141-07*
2.	Standardized root mean square residual (RMR)	0.0149
3.	Goodness of fit index	0.9241
4.	Adjusted goodness-of fit index	0.9133
5.	Comparative fit index	0.9732
6.	Normed fit index	0.9417

*Significant at zero per cent level.

proposed research model is a moderately good Fit to the observed data, since their respective co-efficients are satisfying the standard level of the co-efficients.

Direct, Indirect and Total Effect of Service Quality Factors

The direct and indirect effect of independent variables on the dependent variable (Customer loyalty) have been examined with the help of path co-efficients. The formulated hypotheses in the present are:

Hypotheses

H_1 : There is significant direct impact of basic service on overall attitude towards service provider;

H_2 : There is a significant indirect impact of basic service on customers loyalty through the overall attitude towards service provider;

H_3 : There is a significant direct impact of value added services overall attitude towards service provider;

H_4 : There is a significant indirect impact of value added services on customer loyalty through the overall attitude towards service provider;

H_5 : There is a significant impact of customer care on overall attitude towards service provider;

H_6 : There is a significant impact of customer care on customer loyalty through overall attitude towards service provider;

H_7 : There is a significant impact of responsiveness on overall attitude towards service provider;

H_8 : There is a significant impact of responsiveness on customer loyalty on financial performance through the overall attitude towards service provider

H_9 : There is a significant impact of assurance on overall attitude towards service provider;

H_{10} : There is a significant impact of assurance on customer loyalty overall attitude towards service provider;

H_{11} : There is a significant impact of Recharge on overall, attitude towards service provider;

H_{12} : There is significant impact of recharge on customer loyalty through the overall attitude towards service provider; and

H_{13} : There is a significant impact of overall attitude toward service provider on the customer loyalty.

The direct effect was defined as the standardized path co-efficient for the direct relation between two variables. The indirect effects were defined as a relation between two variables over one or more intermediate variables. The measure of indirect effects was acquired by multiplying standardized path co-efficients, followed by the additional of all path results between two variables. The direct, indirect path co-efficient and the total effect of the independent variables are shown in Table 6.31.

Table 6.31: Direct and Indirect Effect of Service Quality on Customer Loyalty

Hypothesis	Path	Direct effect	Indirect effect	Total effect
H_1	Basic services → overall attitudes	0.3126	0	0.3126
H_2	Basic services → customer loyalty	0.1272	0.1786	0.3058
H_3	Value added services → overall attitude	0.4732	0	0.4732
H_4	Value added services → customer loyalty	0.3082	0.1563	.4645
H_5	Customer care → overall attitude	0.4168	0	0.4168
H_6	Customer care → customer loyalty	0.2717	0.3013	.5420
H_7	Responsiveness → overall attitude	0.3733	0	0.3733
H_8	Responsiveness → customer loyalty	0.1309	0.1257	0.2566
H_9	Assurance → overall attitude	0.4038	0	0.4038
H_{10}	Assurance → customer loyalty	0.1844	0.2962	0.4806
H_{11}	Recharge → overall attitude	0.3142	0	0.3142
H_{12}	Recharge → customer loyalty	0.1014	0.1391	0.2405
H_{13}	Overall attitude → customer loyalty	0.5841	0	0.5841

The strongest effect in the model is from overall attitude to customer loyalty (H_{11}), since its total effect is 0.5841. It is followed by customer care to customer loyalty, since its' total effect is 0.5420. It reveals that the customer care has both direct and indirect impact on customer loyalty (0.2717+0.3013). In fact the indirect on customer loyalty is higher than its direct effect. When the company is focusing on the customer loyalty, it has to consider more on the customer care among their customers and also their perception on overall attitude towards the service provider.

In the case of basic services, the direct effect on customer loyalty is only 0.1272, whereas, its' indirect effect through the overall attitude towards service provider is 0.1786. It infers that the focus should be on the basic services to overall attitude and then to customers loyalty. Similar trend is noticed in the case of effect of customer care, assurance and recharge, whereas, the indirect effect is higher than its direct effect. Therefore, the structures and potentials inherent in an overall perception on service providers are six requisites for burning an commonly understood responsiveness into customer loyalty for the Company. The other independent variable relevant for the customer loyalty of the company is customer care and assurance.

REFERENCES

1. Dekimpe, M.G., Steenkamp, J.B.E.M., Mellens, M., and Abeele, P.v (1991), "Decline and variability in brand loyalty", *International Journal of Research in Marketing*, 14 (1) pp.405-420.
2. Ganesh, J., Arnold., M.J., and Reynolds, K.E (2000), "Understanding the customer base of service providers: an examination of the difference between swtichers and stayers", *Journal of Marketing,* 64(2), July, pp.65-87.
3. Serkan Aydin and Gokhan Ozer (2005), "The analysis of antecedents of customer loyalty in the Turtish mobile telecommunication market", *European Journal of Marketing,* 39(7 & 8), pp.910-923.
4. Oliver, R.L. (1999), "When customer loyalty?", *Journal of Marketing,* 63(Special issue), pp.33-44.
5. Ehrenberg, A.S.S.\ (1998), Repeat buying. Facts, Theory and Application, Oxford University Press, Oxford.
6. Fournier, S and Yao, J.C. (1997), "Reviving brand loyalty: a conceptualization in than the frame work of consumer-hand relationship", *International Journal of Research in Marketing,* 14 (15), pp.451-472.
7. Farley, J.U. (1964), "Why does Brand Loyalty' very over products?", *Journal of Marketing Research,* 1(4), pp.9-14.
8. Brown, G.H (1952), "Brand Loyalty- Fact or Fiction?", Advertising Age, 23(1), pp.53-55.
9. Boulding, W. Kalra A, Staelin, R and Zeithaml, V.A (1993), "A Dynamic process model of service Qualtiy: four Expectation to Behavioural intentions", *Journal of Marketing Research,* 30(February), pp.7-27.
10. Narayandas, N., (1996), "The link between customer satisfaction and customer loyalty: An Empirical Investigation", Working paper, No: 97-017, Harvard Business school, Boston, MA.
11. Kim, M. Park, M and Jeong, D., (2004), "The effects of customer satisfaction and switching barrier on customer loyalty in korean mobile telecommunication services", *Telecommunication Policy,* 28(2), pp.145-159.
12. Gerpost, T, Rams W and Schindler, A (2001), "Customer Retention, Loyalty, and satisfaction policy", 25(4), pp.249-269.
13. Lee, M and cunninghan, L.F (2001), "A cost/Benefit Approach to understanding service Loyalty", *Journal of services marketing.* 15(2), pp.113-130.
14. Chadha, S.K and Deepa Kapoor, (2009), "Effect of switching cost, service quality and customer satisfaction on customer loyalty of cellular service providers in Indian.
15. Ashish Dash (2007), "Changes in usage price of cellular phone services and its welfare implications fort eh subscribers: An evidence from India", *South Asian Journal of Management,* 14 (1), pp.17-35.

16. Child, J and Faulkner, D., (1988), "*Strategies of Corporation: Managing Alliances, Net Works and Joint Ventures,* Oxford University Press, Oxford. University Press, Oxford.
17. Gulati, R., (1998), "Alliances and Networks', *Strategic Management Journal,* 19(4), pp.293-317.
18. Serkan Aydin and Gokhan Ozer (2004), "The analysis of antecedents of customer loyalty in the Furkish mobile Telecommunication market", *European Journal of Marketing,* 39(7&8), pp.910-925.
19. Klaus, Moeher (2009), "Intangible and Financial Performance. Causes and Effects", *Journal of Intellectual Capital,* 10(20), pp. 224-245.

Summary of Findings, Conclusion and Recommendation

Introduction

The present Study is classified into three important parts. The first part covers the profile of the customers and the factors influencing to have the mobile phone service in GSM Market. It is followed by the second part, which includes the service quality of the service providers and customers satisfaction in the GSM Market. The third part of the Study analyses the switching behaviours customer loyalty in the GSM Market.

The present Study confines its objectives: (i) to reveal the profile of the customers in GSM mobile service market; (ii) to identify the Factors influencing to select the service providers; (iii) to evaluate the service quality offered by various service providers; (iv) to examine the service quality gap among the customers; (v) to show the customers satisfaction and its correlates; (vi) to evaluate the impact of service quality on the overall attitude towards the service provider in GSM Market; and (vii) to identify the switching behaviour and customer loyalty and its antecedents consequences in GSM Market.

In order to fulfill the objectives of the Research, the present Study selects the Kanniya Kumari District purposively. Based on the population of the 13 Blocks in the District, the sample was determined. In total, a sample of 4 per 10,000 population in each Block of the District is selected as the sample. The total sample size came to 924. Out of 924, the fully responded customers for the interview schedule is 693. Out of 693, the customers of Airtel, Aircel, BSNL, Vodafone, Idea and Others have been included for the Study, since other service providers are playing a very minimum role among the customers in the present Study area. Finally, the included sample size came to 693. The data collected from the customers were processed with help of appropriate statistical tools. The analysis and interpretations were discussed in the previous Chapter. In this Chapter, the Summary of Findings, Conclusions and Policy Implications are presented.

Summary of Findings

The important age group among the customers is 25 to 35 years. In the present Study, the customers, with the age of 35 and less than 35 years, is grouped as youngsters, whereas, the customers with the age of above 35 years, is treated as elders. The number of young customers is greater than the elder customers in the Study Area.

The important service provider among the customers is BSNL and Airtel. The most important service provider among the young customer is Airtel, whereas, the elder customers, it is BSNL. The dominant gender among the young and old customers is male.

The dominant level of education among the customers is undergraduation and postgraduation. The most important level of education among the young and old customers is undergraduation. The important marital status among the customers is married and unmarried. The most important marital status among the youngsters is unmarried, whereas, among the elders, it is 'married'.

The important occupation among the customers is private employment and studentship. The most important occupation among the young and old customers is studentship and private employment, respectively. The dominant family size among the customers is 3 to 4 and 5 to 6 members. The most important family size among the young and old customers is 5 to 6 and 3 to 4 members, respectively.

The important personal income per month among the customers is Rs.12,001 to 16,000 and above 16,000. The most important personal income among the young and old customers is Rs.8,001 to 12,000 and above Rs.16,000 per month, respectively. The dominant number of earning members per family among the customers is two and one. The most important number of earning members per family among the young and old customers is two and one, respectively.

The important family income among the customers is Rs.18,001 to 24,000 per month and Rs.12,001 to 18,000. The most important family income per month among the young customers is Rs.12,001 to 18,000, whereas, among the elder customers, it is Rs.18,001 to 24,000.

The important level of sociability among the customers is 3.00 to 4.00 and above 4.00, which indicates moderate to high. The most important level of sociability among the young customers is high, whereas, among the old customers, it is moderate. The important level of media exposure among the customers is high and moderate. The most important level of media exposure among the young customers is high, whereas, among the old customers, it is moderate.

The dominant level of innovativeness among the customers is moderate and high. The level of innovativeness among the youngsters is slightly greater than among the elder customers. The important level of scientific orientation among the customers is low and very low. The most important level of innovativeness among the young and old customers is low. The level of innovativeness among the young customers is greater than among the old customers.

The important level of risk orientation among the customers is moderate and low. The most important level of risk orientation among the young and old customers is moderate and very low, respectively. The level of risk orientation among the old customers is very poor, compared to young customers. In total, the personality traits of the customers are low and moderate. The most important level of personality among the young and old customers is low and very low. The level of personality among the young customers is lesser than among the old customers.

The discriminant number of mobile phone used at the household of customers is two and one. The most important number of mobile phones among the young and old customers' household is two and one, respectively. The important brand of handset preferred by the customers is Nokia, which is commonly seen among the young and old customers.

The important purpose of using cell phone services among the young customers is symbol of status, convenience and multi-purpose, whereas, among the old customers, these are official, STD calls and low cost. Regarding the perception on purpose of using cell phone services, the significant difference among the two group of customers has been noticed in the case of perception on official, status symbol, low cost, STD calls, dissatisfaction with landline and multi-purpose.

Thc dominant source of important service providers among the young customers is distributors, salesmen and retailers, whereas, among the old customers, these are advertisement, company and promotional measures. Regarding the importance given on the sources of information, the significant difference among the young and old customers has been noticed in the perception on salesmen, advertisement, company, retailers and distributors.

The highly perceived variables leading to choose the service providers among the young customers is network coverage, low cost SIM card and voice clarity, whereas, old customers, these are inter-network coverage, free incoming facility and national roaming facility. Regarding the perception on the variables leading to choose, the significant difference among the two group of customers have been identified in the case of free incoming facility, nominal changes on calls, network coverage, free SMS facility, prepaid/post paid facility, low cost SIM card, land image, inter network coverage, low activation charges, multi-media messaging facility, positive word of mouth and special/festival offers.

The important factors leading to choose the service provider narrated by the factor analysis are service, economy, coverage, schemes and image. The important variables in 'service' are free SMS facility and lesser official formalities, whereas, in the case of 'economy' factor, these are low cost SIM card and nominal charges on calls. In the case of 'coverage' factor, the important variables are network coverage and inter-network coverage.

The important variables in the 'schemes' factor are frequent schemes and increased validity period, whereas, in the case of 'image', these variables are goodwill of the service provider and brand image. The included variables in each factor explain it to a reliable extent.

The highly perceived factors leading to choose the service provider narrated by the factor analysis are service, economy, coverage, schemes and image. The important variables in 'service' are free SMS facility and lesser official formalities, whereas, in the case of 'economy' factor, these are low cost SIM card and nominal changes on calls. In the case of 'coverage' factor, the important variables are network coverage and inter-network coverage.

The important variables in the 'schemes' factor is frequent schemes and increased validity period, whereas, in the case of 'image', these variables are goodwill of the service provider and brand image. The included variables in each factor explain it to a reliable extent.

The highly perceived factors leading to choose the service provider among the young customers is schemes and economy, whereas, among the old customers, these are coverage and service. Regarding the perception on the factors, the significant difference among the two group of customers has been identified in the case of perception on service, economy, coverage, and schemes.

The important factors perceived by the customers of Airtel and Aircel are service and coverage, whereas, among the customers of BSNL, these two are coverage and economy. Among the customers of Vodafone, these two factors are economy and service, whereas, among the customers of Idea, the two factors are schemes and service. Among the customers of Others, these two factors are coverage and schemes. Regarding the perception on factors, the significant difference among the different group of customers has been identified in all factors except the customers.

The significantly associating important profile of the customers on their perception on the factors leading to choose their service providers is their personality score, family income, number of earning members per family, personal income and age of the customers. The important discriminative factors among the young and old customers are service and schemes. The 'service' is highly perceived by old customers, whereas the, 'schemes' is highly perceived by young customers.

The important service quality factors of the service provider in GSM Market is identified as Basic Services, Value Added Services, Customer Care, Responsiveness, Assurance and Recharge. The important variables in Basic services are quick activation of number and connecting calls easily. In the Value Added Services, these variables are long options for dialer and tunes facility of getting missed. In the case of Customer Care, these first two variables are performing right, since the first time and maintain arrow-free records.

The important variables in responsiveness is willingness to help customers and telling customers exactly what services will be provided, whereas, in the case of assurance factor, the first two variables are employee are consistently courteous and customers feel comfortable, interacting with employees. In the case of 'recharge' factor, the variables are 'e' recharge and various options in recharging coupons. The variables included in each service quality factors explain it to a reliable extent.

The highly perceived Service Quality Factors (SQFs) among the young customers is recharge and customer care, whereas, among the old customers, the two are value added services and recharge. The highly expected SQFs among the young customers are basic services and customer care, whereas, among the old customers, these are customer care and recharge.

The service quality gap among the customers of all service providers are identified as negative. It reveals that the customers are not satisfied upto their level of expectation. Regarding the service quality gap, the significant difference among the customers of various service providers has been identified.

There is a significant difference among the young and old customers, regarding their mean difference in all service quality gap. The higher discriminant power is identified in the case of assurance gap and customer care gap. The important discriminant service quality gap among the two groups of customers is the customer care gap and assurance gap.

The significantly associating important profile variables with the service quality gap of the customers are their personality score, family income, number of earning members per family, personal income, level of education and age of the customers.

The overall attitude towards the service provider among the customers has been measured with the help of eleven variables. The high variables related to overall attitude towards service provider among the young customers is voice clarity and plan options, whereas, among the old customers, these are clarity of signals and coverage of the network. Regarding the perception on the variables related to the overall attitude, the significant difference among the two group of customers has been identified in the case of plan options, service quality, basic services, value added services, coverage of the network, and voice clarity.

The important variables in the overall attitude is connectivity and service quality. The included eleven variables explain the overall attitude towards the service provider to a reliable extent. The important level of overall attitude among the customers is high and low. Among the young and old customers, the most important overall attitude is high. The overall attitude towards the service provider is identified among the customers of Idea and BSNL. There is a significant difference among the customers of various service providers regarding their overall attitude. The significantly associating profile variables with the overall attitude among the customers is their age, level of education, personal income, number of earning members per family, family income, and personality score.

The higher level of expectation on SQFs has been noticed among the customers of Idea and Others. The significant mean difference among the satisfied and dissatisfied customers is identified in the case of basic services, value added services and customer care. The higher discriminant power is identified in the case of value added services and customer care. The important discriminant expectation among the two group of customers is customer care and value added services, which are identified as higher among the 'dissatisfies' than the 'satisfies'.

The overall perception on SQFs is identified as higher among the customer of Idea and Vodafone. The significant mean difference among the 'satisfies' and 'dissatisfies' has been noticed in the perception on basic services, value added services, customer care, responsiveness, assurance and recharge. The higher discriminant power is noticed in the case of value added services and customer care. The important discriminate perception on SQFs among the 'satisfies' and 'dissatisfies' are customer care and value added services, which are higher among the 'satisfies' than the 'dissatisfies'.

The discirminant validity among the service quality factors have been confirmed, since the Average Variance Extracted by the SQFs are greater than the sum of square of correlation coefficient between the respective SQF with other SQFs. The significantly and positively influencing SQFs an overall attitude towards the service provider among the youngsters is basic services, value added services, responsiveness, assurance and recharge.

Among the old customers, the significantly influencing SQFs on the overall attitude towards the service provider is basic services, customer care, responsiveness, and assurance. The change in perception on SQFs explains the charges in overall attitude towards the service provider and identified as higher among the young customers than the old customers.

The significantly and positively influencing SQFs on the overall, attitude towards Airtel among the customers, is basic services, responsiveness and assurance, whereas, among the customers, is Aircel. These SQFs are basic services, customer care, responsiveness, and recharge. Among the customers of BSNL, these SQFs are basic services, customer care, responsiveness and recharge, whereas, among the customers of Vodafone, these SQFs are basic services, customer care, responsiveness and recharge. The significantly influencing SQFs, among the customers of Idea, are basic services, customer care, responsiveness and assurance, whereas, among the customer care and recharge, is.

Most of the customers are having a higher switching intention from the existing service provider. The switching intention is identified as higher among the young than the old customers. Regarding the switching intention of the customer of various service providers, the important rate of switching intention is very high. Only few customers are having lesser intention of switching from the existing service provider.

The important factors leading to switching among the customer have been examined with the help of Exploratory Factor Analysis. These factors are switching cost, service quality, pricing structure, network and environment. The important variables in switching cost is lesser switching cost and comparative advantage, whereas, in the 'service quality' factor, the important variables are excellent service and value – added service.

The important variables in 'pricing structure' are discount and free incoming, whereas, in the case of 'Network' factor, these variables are network and connecting. In the case of environment factor, the important variables are friends and relatives; and popularity in the market. The included variables in each factor explain it to a reliable extent.

The highly perceived switching factors among the young customers are service quality and network, whereas, among the old customers, these factors are switching cost and price structure. Regarding the perception on the factors leading to switching, the significant difference among the young and old customers has been noticed in the case of switching cost, service quality, price structure, network and environment.

The highly viewed switching factors among the customers of Airtel are price structure and switching cost, whereas, among the customers of Aircel, these factors are price structure and switching cost. Among the customers of BSNL, the important switching factors are price structure and network, whereas, among the customers of Vodafone, these are price structures and switching costs. The important switching factors among the customers of Idea are service quality and network, whereas, among the customers of Others, these are switching cost and service quality. Regarding the perception on switching factors, the significant difference among the customers of various service providers has been identified in the case of all five factors.

The significantly associating important profile variables with the perception on switching factors among the customer are their personality score, number of earning members per family, family income and personal income. The significant mean difference among the young and old customers have been noticed in the case of all five switching factors. The higher discriminant power of the factor is noticed in the case of price structure and service quality. The important discriminant switching factors are price structure and service quality.

The discriminant validity among the switching factors has been confirmed, since the Average Variance Extracted by each factor is greater than the sum of square of correlation coefficient between the factor with other factors. The significantly and positively influencing switching on the switching intention among the young customers is their service quality and network. Among the old customers, the significantly and positively influencing switching factors on switching intention are switching cost, price structure, network and environment.

The significantly and positively influencing switching factors on switching intentions among the customers of Airtel are switching cost and price structure, whereas, among the customers of Aircel, these are switching cost, service quality network. Among the custmers of BSNL, the significantly and positively influencing switching factors on switching intentions are switching cost and price structure, whereas, among the customers of Vodafone and Others, these factors are switching cost, service quality, price structure and network. Among the customers of Idea, the significantly and positively influencing switching factors on the switching intentions are switching cost and service quality.

By the comparative analysis on the overall attitude towards service provider and the switching among the customers, the analysis identified that there is no guarantee of poor switching intention, because of higher overall attitude towards the service provider. Majority of the customers with higher overall attitude towards the service provider are having a higher switching intention.

The significant mean difference among the 'satisfies' and 'dissatisfies' has been identified in the switching factors; namely, switching cost, service quality, price structure and network. The higher discriminant power has been identified in the case of switching cost and price structure. The important switching factors among the 'satisfies' and 'dissatisfies' is price structure and network, which are identified as higher among the 'dissatisfies' than the 'satisfies'.

The customer loyalty has been measured with the help of 10 variables. The highly perceived variables among the young customers are service differentiation from my service provider and competitive advantage from any service provider and recommend any service provider to others. The important level of customer loyalty among the customers is very poor. Among both old and young customers, the customer loyalty is lesser.

Even though, the customer loyalty is lesser among the customers, it is very poor among the customers of Vodafone and Airtel. Regarding the customer loyalty, there is no significant difference among the customers of various service providers. The significantly associating important profile variables with the customer loyalty among the customers, are, age, level of education, personal income, number of earning members per family, family income and personality.

The analysis of the overall attitude towards service providers and customer loyalty in the GSM reveals that there is no guarantee of customer loyalty among the customers who are satisfied and highly satisfied. Even the highly satisfied customers are poor and very poor in customer loyalty.

The significantly and negatively influencing switching factors on the customer loyalty among the young customers are the switching cost and price structure, whereas, among the old customers, these factors are also the same. The changes in the importance given on the switching factor explain the charges in the customer loyalty to a greater extent among the young customers than the old customers.

The significantly and negatively influencing switching factors on the customer loyalty among the customers of Airtel are switching cost, service quality and price structure, whereas, among the customers of Aircel, it is switching cost, price structure and network. Among the customers of BSNL, these factors are switching cost and price structure, whereas, among the customers of Vodafone, these switching factors are switching cost, service quality, price structure and network. Among the customers of Idea, these factors are switching cost, network, and environment, whereas, among the customers of Others, these factors are switching cost, price structure and environment.

The higher direct effect of service quality factors on customer loyalty has been identified with the case of value added services, customer care and assurance, whereas, the indirect effect through the overall attitude is identified as higher among the customer care and assurance. The overall total effect on customer loyalty is identified as higher by the overall attitude and customer care.

Policy Implications

The service quality of the service providers in GSM is still not upto the level of customers' expectation. Hence, the service providers are advised to analyse the customers' expectation in a detailed manner and mould their delivery of service at par with their customer. For that purpose, they have to set up so many customers Research Cells in all Circles, then only they can implement appropriate service strategy in GSM Market.

Better customer care services and strong network range are most important for retaining the customers in the case of mobile services. Though attaractive offers may help to attract certain customers, yet it may not help to retain those customers without proper customer care and service features. Thus customer service should strengthen the Customer Care Departments and develop service features, especially, a strong network, for satisfying and retaining customers in the long run.

Since the customer loyalty is very poor among the customers in GSM Market, each service provider is advised to generate the appropriate marketing strategy to create a customer loyalty among their customers, since the cost of retaining existing customers is lesser than the cost of acquiring new customers. It is almost a common recommendation to all service providers, since there is no significant difference among the various service providers regarding their customer loyalty.

The Market competition in the Mobile Phone Service Market will inevitably become much more intensive, since India's formal entry into the WTO. More and more foreign giants will get involved in due course. On the other hand, it is expected that the newly restructured Telecom Service in India, BSNL will play an important role in Mobile Phone Service. Therefore, Firms expecting to build and maintain competitive advantage in this Market must try their best to improve their service quality, deliver superior customer value, achieve higher customer satisfaction and turn behaviour intensions of customers into the true purchasing behaviuor.

The service providers should focus on all service quality variables, namely, tangibility, responsiveness, reliability, empathy and quality service to prepare their marketing strategy. This should sweat vigorously meet rising level of customers satisfaction that ushers in superior customer value.

Since the loyalty programses accompanied by well-designed customer satisfaction programmes can be effective in increasing customer retention, the service providers pay more attention on these aspects.

The design of proper incentives can be achieved by analyzing customers' evaluation of different satisfaction components and usage patterns. Both can help a marketing strategy that combines various promotion tools. For example, in the mobile phone service market, such tools might include more attractive weekend pricing, a new handset with discounted price, and free value-added service for heavy users.

The service providers are better off implementing a feature-based differentiation of service products than using a typical price discrimination scheme. It was also interesting to find that mobile-focus is less sensitive to the pricing aspects of services. In other words, the level of satisfaction on pricing was much less significant for heavy users than for regular users. They seem to look for a good range of supporting services and are willing to pay for them.

Developing and maintaining a loyal customer base is viewed single most important driver of long-term financial performance. It is very important for mobile operators to develop well-designed customer satisfaction programmes for increased customer retention. By analyzing changes in consumption volume and usage patterns, they can provide appropriate incentives at the right time.

The service providers should develop products/services which fulfill the fundamental needs and motives among various customer segments and continuously emphasize this in the communication targeted at the various customer segments. This will provide the best starting point for developing and designing new mobile phone services and then use this as an element in the marketing and communication towards the segments. In this way, the service providers can position their service as a symbol of certain life styles, norms and values that are attractive in the eyes of various segments.

It is becoming an industry-wide belief that the best core marketing strategy for the future is to try to retain existing customers by heightening customer loyalty and customer value. The operators should decrease their subscribers' sensitivity of price. It can be said that factors, such as, trust, perceived service quality, perceived switching cost and positive corporate image are very important for the operators to establish a loyal customer base and decrease their sensitivity to price.

Changing shifts from price and core services to value added service in the market, the operators should differentiate their services and guarantee quality of their services in order to maintain their market share. The differentiated services and the superior quality standards of these services will not only increase trust in the operator, but also enable the formation of a positive corporate image in the subscribers' minds.

In the current business scenario, Mobile Customer Relationship Management (CRM) applications effectively enable service providers to automate business process that involves employees, who spend much of their time out of the office. The use of mobile CRM is mostly benefiting the sales team of the service provider.

The service providers should maximize service quality and customer satisfaction in order to enhance customer loyalty. Service provider must focus on customer oriented service to heighten customer satisfaction. Service providers must concentrate their efforts on improving network quality, pricing and value added services. Switching costs contribute to increased loyalty and customer retention; therefore cellular service providers can implement some reward programs to increase the benefits of subscription, and provide variety of recharge top-ups helping the customers to reduce call and SMS rates, which results in loyalty inertia.

The customer focus may be improved with the help of technological advancement of Customers Relationship Management (CRM). It includes the implementation of self service options, reminder when bills are due;

feedback about product or service; staff contact personnel have all the relevant information to deal with the issue; customer satisfaction; profitable relationship; competitive advantage; number of customers; measure your customers' value; revenue per customer and order fulfillment process.

In addition, to specific service enhancements, service providers should consider more general promotional initiatives, such as, those that producers of mobile services have launched to familiarize consumers with mobile service delivery. The service providers should devote their attention on the simple usage of mobile phone service to the customers.

Nowadays, rural telecommunication has been a significant area, where the service providers can extract the untapped potential customers. It can be emphasized to bring down the widening gap between the urban and rural tele-density. An appropriate rural marketing strategy should be designed by the service providers, since the profile rural customers are differing from urban customers. Apart from the formal media like newspaper, television, radio, cinema and direct mail, rural-specific promotion methods like demonstrations, puppet shows, house-to-house campaigns, processions, rural melas, dance programmes, etc. would be more useful in drawing the attention of rural customers.

The customers' loyalty should be classified into trapped, true loyalty, wanderers and purchased loyalists. The mapping of customer loyalty is presented below:

Customer Loyalty		Customer satisfaction: Low	Customer satisfaction: High
	High	Trapped	True Loyalists
	Low	Wanderers	Purchased Loyalists

For the trapped category of customers, better understanding of causes of their dissatisfaction and responding to their needs can help the service providers to move their customers to high levels of satisfaction. For wanderers, the service providers have to improve the quality of service, focus on speedy solution of their customers' complaints. Further, the loyalty among the customers may be developed by the announcement of special discounts and reward programs. For the purchased loyalists, the service provider has to deliver innovative services regarding value addition and cost of switching to enrich their loyalty. For the true loyalists, the service providers are advised to keep up more inter personal relations.

The service providers are advised to deal with the young and old customer in a careful way. The level of customer loyalty is very low among the young customers eventhough they are satisfied towards their service provider.

The relationship established in the youth has a positive impact on loyalty later in life. Creating a relation to youth is a long-term investment that should build on a profound understanding of youth and their needs and motives. The service providers should develop products/services, which fulfill the fundamental needs and motives among the young customers and continuously emphasise this in the communication targeted at the young customers.

Conclusion

The present Study concludes that the important service quality factors in GSM Market is basic services, value added services, customer care, responsiveness, assurance and recharge. The perception on the above-said factors among the customers is not at their level of expectation. The service quality gap has a significant negative impact on the overall attitude towards the service providers. The switching intentions among the customers are high, whereas, the customer loyalty is very low in the GSM Market. The significantly influencing switching factors on the switching intention among the customers are switching cost, service quality, network and environment. The level of expectation and perception on service quality factors, factors leading to switching intentions, and customer loyalty are different among the young and old customers in the GSM Market. Hence, the Study identifies the need of appropriate marketing strategy to develop the customer loyalty to the nature of market segment.

Direction for Further Research

On the basis of the review of the present study, following areas for further research are proposed;

- The casual relationship between the service quality customer value, customer satisfaction, loyalty and retention for cellular mobile services.
- The linkage between switching cost, customer satisfaction and customer loyalty in the mobile phone service market.
- Demographic discriminators of service quality, switching and customer loyalty in the mobile communication industry.
- The predictors of the customers' expectation on service quality in the mobile phone service market.
- The role of promotional measures in the mobile communication industry.
- Consumer behaviour in cellular phone service market: A market segmentation analysis, and
- Marketing strategies of companies in GSM Market: A customers perspective analysis.

Bibliography

BOOKS

Child, J and Faulkner, D., (1988), "Strategies of Corporation: Managing Alliances, Net Works and Joint Ventures, Oxford University Press, Oxford. University Press, Oxford.

Clarie Selltiz and others, (1962), "Research methods in social sciences.

Kim, M., Park, M, and Jeong, D. (2004), "The effects of customer satisfaction and snitching barriers on customer loyalty in Korean mobile Telecommunication Services", Telecommunication Policy, 28(2).

Leiser, Band Vance, C. (2001), "Cross-national assessment of service quality in the telecommunication industry: evidence from the USA and Germany", Managing Service Quality, 11(5).

Nautiyal Jyoti (1999), "A study on consumer perception of service quality with special reference to RPG cell com and Reliance Telecom", Unpublished Major Project Report, PIMR, Indore.

Oliver, R.C. (1993), "A conceptual Model of Service Quality and Service Satisfaction: Compatible Goals, different concepts", in Swantz, T.A., Bowen, D.E and Brown, SW (Eds). Advances in Marketing and Management, JAI Press, Inc., Green inch, Co-efficient.

Rust, R.T., and Oliver, R.L. (1994), "Service Quality: Insights and Managerial Implications from the Frontier", in Rust, R.T. and Oliver, R.L., (Eds.) Service Quality: New Directions in Theory and Practice, Sage Publications, Thousand Oaks, CA.

Singh, S. (1986), Statistical Techniques in Agricultural Research, Oxford and IBH Publishing Co., New Delhi.

JOURNALS

Ahmed, Z., Johnson, J., Ling, C.P., Fang, T.W and Hui, A.K. (2002), "Country-of-origin and Brand effects on consumer's Evaluations of cruise Lines", International Marketing Review, 19, 2&3).

Alok Mittal and Prerna Sirohi, (2007), "Factor Affecting, Selection of Cell Services: A Cross-Segmental Study", Synergy, 4 (1).

Anderson, E.W., Fornell, C. and Leomann, D.R., (1994), "Customer Satisfaction, Market Share and Profitability: Findings from Sweden", Journal of Marketing, 58 (3), pp.53-66.

Andreassen, T.W. (2000), "Antecedents to Satisfaction with Service Recovery", European Journal of Marketing, 34 (1&2).

Anita Seth, Kiran Momaya and Gupta, H.M. (2005), "An Exploratory Investigation of Customer Loyalty and Retention in Cellular Mobile Communication", Journal of Services Research, Special Issue, December.

Ashish Dash (2007), "Changes in usage price of cellular phone services and its welfare implications fort eh subscribers: An evidence from India", South Asian Journal of Management, 14(1).

Babakus and Roller, G.W(1992), "An empirical assessment of the SERVQUAL scale", Journal of Business Research, 24(3).

Balasubramanian, Paterson and Jarvenpaa, S.L. (2000), "Exploring the implications of M-convenience for markets and marketing", Journal of the Academy of Marketing Science, 30(3), pp.348-361.

Banumathy, S. and Kalaivani, (2006), "Customers' Attitude Towards Cell Phone Services in Communication System", Indian Journal of Marketing, 36(30.

Bearden, W.O. and Teel, J.E., (1983), "Selected Determinants of Consumer satisfaction and complaint reports", Journal of Marketing Research, Vol. 20.

Bearder, W.O. and Teel, J.E. (1983), "Selected Determinants of Consumer Satisfaction and Complaints Reports", Journal of Marketing Research, 20.

Bebko, C.P (2000), "Service Intangibility and its Impact on Consumer Expectations of Service Quality", Journal of Services Marketing, 14(1).

Beltman, J.R., (1974), "A others hold model of attribute satisfaction decision", Journal of Consumer Research, Vol.1, September.

Bettman, J.R., (1974), "A mcohod model of attribute satisfaction decision", Journal of Consumer Research, Vol. I, September.

Carman, J.M., (1990), "Consumer Perceptions of Service quality: An Assessment of SERVQUAL Dimensions", Journal of Retailing, 66(1).

Chada, S.K and Deepa Kapoor (2009), "Effect of Switching Cost, Service Quality and Customer Satisfaction on Customer Loyalty of Cellular Service Providers in Indian Market", The ICFAI University Journal of Marketing Management, 8(1).

Chadha, S.K and Deepa Kapoor, (2009), "Effect of switching cost, service quality and customer satisfaction on customer loyalty of cellular service providers in Indian.

Chao, P and Gupta, P.B. (1995), "Information search and Efficiency of consumer choices of New car: Country of origin effects", International Marketing Review, 12(6).

Chinnadurai, M and Kalpana, B., (2006), "Promotional Strategies of Cellular Services: A Customer Perspective", Indian Journal of Marketing, 26(5).

Clement, J. (2005), "Service quality Gap Models: A Re-examination and Extension", SMART Journal of Business Management Studies, 1(2), July-December.

Cronin, J.J. and Taylor, S.A. (1992), "Measuring service quality: a re-examination and extension", Journal of Marketing, 58(2).

Cronin, J.J., Brady, M.K. and Hult, T.M. (2000), "Assessing the effects of quality, value, consumer satisfaction on consumer behavioural intentions in service environment", Journal of Retailing, 76 (2).

Crowin, J.J. and Taylor, S.A. (1992), "Measuring Service Quality: are Examination and Extension", Journal of Marketing, 56(3).

Dabholhan, P.A, Shepered C.D and Thorpe, D.I. (200), "A comprehensive Frame Work for Service Quality: and Investigation of Critical Conceptual Measurement issues though a Longitudinal Study", Journal of Retailing, 76 (2).

Daxa C. Gohil (2005), "Customers Preferences in Telecom Industry", Management Trends, 2(1), October – March.

Day, G.S., (1969), "A Two-Dimensional Concept of brand loyalty", Journal of Advertising Research, 9(3).

Dekimpe, M.G., Steenkamp, J.B.E.M., Mellens, M., and Abeele, P.v (1991), "Decline and variability in brand loyalty", International Journal of Research in Marketing, 14 (1).

Dick, S.A., and Basu, K. (1994), "Customer Loyalty: Toward and Integrated Conceptual framework", Journal of the Academy of Marketing Science, 22(2).

Essam E.Ibrahim and Pajaree sothornuopatubr (2006), "Country-of-origin and consumer evaluation of mobile Handsets: A comparative study of Scotland and Thailand", Journal of Consumer Behaviour, 5(1).

Evardson, B.O., and Innger Roos, (2003), "Customer Complaints and Switching Behaviour–A Study of Relationship Dynamics in a Telecommunication Company", Journal of Relationship Marketing, 2(1/2).

Fornell, C. and Wernerfelt, B. (1987), "Defensive marketing strategy by customer complaint management: a theoretical analysis", Journal of Marketing Research, vol. 24, November.

Fournier, S and Yao, J.C. (1997), "Reviving brand loyalty: a conceptualization in than the frame work of consumer-hand relationship", International Journal of Research in Marketing, 14(15).

Francis Sudhahar, K. and Lydia Nutan, (2005), "An Objective Study of Customer Behaviour in BPL Mobile Cellular Ltd", Indian Journal of Marketing, 35(5), May.

Ganesh, J., Arnold, J., and Kristy, E., (2000), "Understanding the Customer base of service providers: An Examination of the differences between Switches and Stayers", Journal of Marketing, 64(3).

Ganesh, J., Arnold., M.J., and Reynolds, K.E (2000), "Understanding the customer base of service providers: an examination of the difference between swtichers and stayers", Journal of Marketing, 64(2), July.

Gerpost, T, Rams W and Schindler, A (2001), "Customer Retention, Loyalty, and satisfaction policy", 25(4).

Gerpost, T.J., Rams, W and Shindler, A. (2001), "Customer retention, loyalty and satisfaction in the German mobile cellular telecommunication market", Telecommunication policy, 25(4).

Gulati, R., (1998), "Alliances and Networks', Strategic Management Journal, 19(4).

Johnson, D. (2001), "Customer Switching Behaviour in on line services: An Exploratory Story", Journal of the Academy of Marketing Science, 29(4).

Kim, M. Park, M and Jeong, D., (2004), "The effects of customer satisfaction and switching barrier on customer loyalty in korean mobile telecommunication services", Telecommunication Policy, 28(2).

Klaus, Moeher (2009), "Intangible and Financial Performance. Causes and Effects", Journal of Intellectual Capital, 10(20).

Lapierre, J. (1996), "Service quality: the construct, the dimensionality, and its measurement", in swartz, T.A., Bower, D.E and Brown, S.W (eds), Advances in services marketing and management, Vol. 5, JAI press Juc., Greenwich, CT.

Lee, J. Lee, and Feick, L. (2001), "The impact of switching costs on the customer satisfaction – loyalty link: Mobile phone service in France", Journal of services marketing, 15(1).

Lee, M and cunninghan, L.F (2001), "A cost/Benefit Approach to understanding service Loyalty", Journal of services marketing. 15(2).

Levilt, T. (1981), "Marketing intangible products and product intangibles", Harvard Business Reviews, 59(3).

Lovelock, C.H. (1983), "Classifying Services to gain Strategic Marketing Insights", Journal of Marketing, 47(3).

Martin Fassnachk and Ibrahim Koese, (2006), "Quality of Electronic Service", Journal of Services Research, 9(1).

Oliver, R.C. (1981), "Measurement and Evaluation of Satisfaction Powers in Retail Settings", Journal of Retailing, 57 (Fall).

Oliver, R.C., (1981), "Measurement and Evaluation of Satisfaction Powers in Retail Settings", Journal of Retailing, 57(Fall).

Oliver, R.L. (1999), "When customer loyalty?", Journal of Marketing, 63(Special issue).

Palkar Apoorva, (2004), "Determinants of customer satisfaction for Cellular Service Providers", Udyaog Pragati, 28(1), January-March.

Parasuraman, A., Zathanl, V.A and beny, L.L. (1988), "SERVQUAL: A Multiple Item Scale for Measuring Consumer Receptions of Service Quality", Journal of Retailing, 64 (Spring).

Parasuraman, A., Zeithaml, V.A. and Berry, C.C. (1988), "SERVQUAL: A multiple–item scale for measuring consumer perceptions of service", Journal of Retailing, 64 (spring).

Parasuraman, A., Zeithammal, V.A. and Berry, L.L. (1988), "SERVQUAL: A multiple item scale for measuring consumer perceptions of service quality", Journal of Retailing, 64(1).

Parasuraman, A., Zeithammal, V.A., and Berry, L.L. (1988), "A conceptual model of service quality and its implications for future research", Journal of Marketing, 49 (Fall).

Peter, J., Churchill, G and Brown, T (1993), "Caution in the use of Difference Sores in Consumer Research", Journal of consumer Research, 19(4).

Peter, J.P. (1981), "Construct Validity: A Review of base Issues and Marketing Practices", Journal of Marketing Research, 18 (May).

Prahad, C.K. and Ramasamy, V. (2000), "Co-opting Customer Competencies", Harvard Business Review, January-February.

Prahad, C.K. and Ramasamy, V., (2000), "Co-operating Customer Competencies" Harvard Business Review, January-February.

Raja, K.G., Uma Sharma and Shashilkala, R., (2006), "Measuring customer satisfaction among mobile Handset End users: AN Empirical Study", The Icfaian Journal of Management Research, February.

Rana Weera, C and Neely, A. (2003), "Some moderating effects on the Service Quality–Customer Retention Link", International Journal of Operations and Production Management, 23(2).

Ray Subhasis and Sarkar Avishek (2006), "Analysing influence of Brand Vis-à-vis. Price in Indian Mobile industry", The ICFAI Journal of Marketing Management, 5(4).

Reichheld, F.F. and Sasser, W.E. (1990), "Zero defections: Quality Comes to Services", Harvard Business Review, September-October.

Revathi, S. and Padmavathy, (2005), "Preferences in Cellular service providers in the post liberalization era", Indian Journal of Marketing, February.

Roos, Inger (2002), "Methods of Investigating Critical Incidents: A Comparative Review", Journal of Services Research, 4(3).

Roos, Inger (2002), "Methods of Investigating Critical Incidents: A Comparative Review", Journal of Service Research, 4(3).

Rust, R.T. and Zahorit, A.J., (1993), "Customer Satisfaction, Customer Retention, and Market Share", Journal of Retailing, 69(2). Summer.

Sasikala, P. (2006), "Telecom Services: Measurement of customer satisfaction", The Icfaian Journal of Management Research, 5(10).

Selvaraj, V.M. and Ganesan Malathi, (2005), "A Study of Consumer Behaviour Towards Cell Phone Users in Thuthookudi city", Indian Journal of Marketing.

Selvarasu, A. Gomathi Shankar, K. and Loganathan, (2006), "GSM Mobile Service in Telecom Sector: An Ontology of Quality of Service", The ICFAI Journal of Service Marketing, 4(4).

Serkan Aydin and Gokhan Ozer (2004), "The analysis of antecedents of customer loyalty in the Furkish mobile Telecommunication market", European Journal of Marketing, 39(7&8).

Serkan Aydin and Gokhan Ozer (2005), "The analysis of antecedents of customer loyalty in the Turtish mobile telecommunication market", European Journal of Marketing, 39(7 & 8).

Shashikumar Sharma, and D.S. Chauley (2007), "Consumer behaviour towards mobile service providers: An Empirical Study", The ICFAI Journal of Marketing Management, 6(1).

Srideshmukh, Jagdip Singh and Barry Sabol (2002), "Consumer Trust, Value and Loyalty in Relational Exchanges", Journal of Marketing, 66.

Srikant, A., (2006), "Cellular Mobile Industry in India: A Study", The ICFAI Journal of Services Marketing, 4(1).

Srivastava, R., Jatin Bhangde, Nivar, Bhatt, Keinal Gogri and Himal Margatia (2006), "Role of Competition in Growing Markets: Telecom Sector", Indian Journal of Marketing, 11(3).

Vijaykumar, R. and Ruthra Priya, P. (2006), "Satisfaction derived by the Airtel subscribers in Coimbatore", Indian Journal of Marketing, 26(10).

Yonggui Wang and Hing, Poto (2002), "Service Quality, Customer Satisfaction and Behaviour Intentions", Journal of Services Marketing, 4(6).

Yonggui Wang and Hung-Polo (2002), "Service Quality, Customer satisfaction and behaviour intentions", Journal of Service Marketing, 41 (6).

Zillur Rahman (2005), "Service quality: Caps in the Indian Banking Industry", The ICFAI Journal of Marketing Management.

PROJECT REPORT

Agarwal Pradeep (1999), "Comparison of customer satisfaction level of RPG and Reliance Telecom customers", Unpublished major Project Report, PIMR, Indore.

WEBSITE

www. Supercommindia 2004. com/Indian_t_sehtm (2002 figures).

http// www.emeraldinsight. Com / 1463-6697. html.

Index